W9-AVC-257

MY
TURN
TO
SPEAK

We wish to thank Zahra Bani-Sadr and Ahmad Salamatian for their invaluable assistance.

MY TURN TO SPEAK

Iran, the Revolution & Secret Deals with the U.S.

Abol Hassan Bani-Sadr

from a series of interviews by
Jean-Charles Deniau

FOREWORD BY
Ambassador L. Bruce Laingen

BRASSEY'S (US), INC.

A Macmillan Publishing Company

WASHINGTON • NEW YORK • LONDON
OXFORD • BEIJING • FRANKFURT • SÃO PAULO
SYDNEY • TOKYO • TORONTO

Original title of the French edition—*Le complot des ayatollahs*
Copyright © 1989 Editions La Découverte, 1 place Paul-Painlevé,
75005 Paris.

English-language edition © 1991 by Brassey's (US), Inc.
Translated by William Ford

BRASSEY'S (US), Inc.

Editorial Offices
Brassey's (US), Inc.
8000 Westpark Drive
First Floor
McLean, Virginia 22102

Order Department
Brassey's Book Orders
c/o Macmillan Publishing Co.
Front and Brown Streets
Riverside, New Jersey 08075

Brassey's (US), Inc., books are available at special discounts for bulk
purchases for sales promotions, premiums, fund-raising, or educational use
through the Special Sales Director, Macmillan Publishing Company, 866
Third Avenue, New York, New York 10022.

British Library Cataloguing in Publication Data
Bani-Sadr, Abol Hassan
   My turn to speak : Iran, the revolution & secret deals with the U.S.
   1. Iran, history
   I. Title   II. Deniau, Jean-Charles   III. Complot des ayatollahs. *English*
   955.054

   ISBN   0-08-040563-0

Library of Congress Cataloging-in-Publication Data
Bani Sadr, Abu al-Hasan.
   [Complot des ayatollahs. English]
   My turn to speak : Iran, the revolution & secret deals with the U.S. /
Abol Hassan Bani-Sadr ; from a series of interviews by Jean-Charles
Deniau ; foreword by L. Bruce Laingen.
      p.   cm.
   Translation of: Le complot des ayatollahs.
   Includes index.
   ISBN   0-08-040563-0
   1. Iran-Iraq War, 1980-1988—Diplomatic history. 2. Iran—Politics
and government—1979- 3. United States—Foreign relations—
Iran. 4. Iran—Foreign relations—United States.
   I. Deniau, Jean-Charles.   II. Title.
   DS318.85.B3613   1991
   955.05'4—dc20   90-48212
                                                                 CIP

10   9   8   7   6   5   4   3   2
Published in the United States of America
Design by Robert Bull Design.

CONTENTS

CONTENTS

•

•

CONTENTS

•

The Diplomatic Yo-yo • The Fatal Blow

FOREWORD

The invitation by the publisher at Brassey's (US) to evaluate this book by Abol Hassan Bani-Sadr, published earlier in France, brought back for me a flood of memories. I had known of Bani-Sadr during my assignment in 1979 as chargé d'affaires in the U.S. embassy in Tehran. And of course I knew him even better—however indirectly—when I became the senior American diplomat held hostage during the 444 days that followed the seizure of the embassy on November 4, 1979. After reading the manuscript, I felt that it was important to publish *My Turn to Speak* as a detailed insider's look at the Iranian revolution, the Ayatollah Khomeini, the hostage crisis, and the Iran-Iraq war.

That in no way suggests that the U.S. publisher or I draw the same conclusions that Bani-Sadr does, nor do we feel that his evidence is always convincing. Readers must draw their own conclusions. I join with the publisher in reminding the reader that Bani-Sadr's allegations about behind-the-scenes roles played by President Carter, candidate and then President Reagan, and candidate and then President Bush have been publicly denied by these three distinguished American leaders and their staffs. Rumors about these roles have all been carefully and heavily investigated by prominent American and international media reporters. No one, to my knowledge, has yet found conclusive evidence to support Bani-Sadr's sometimes sensational accusations. Very simply, readers must accept the book for what it is— a personal, obviously self-serving, but very important view of a major event in world history.

What is valuable about this book is the portrait only Bani-Sadr could paint of his days in Paris and Iran as one of Ayatollah Khomeini's closest advisers and, later, as a growing opponent of the path taken by the revolution. Of equal interest is Bani-Sadr's description of an Iran in constant turmoil, full of intrigues centered around Khomeini. He describes a country of fragmented power, an Iran where the Ayatollah never had the total control that those outside Iran thought he had. Finally, the reader sees, from Bani-Sadr's position as head of state, his view of the causes of the Iran-Iraq war and of the way the war was conducted— particularly the struggles between the Iranian professional military, the mullahs, and the Revolutionary Guards.

Bani-Sadr writes how appalled he was by the way that infighting among Iranian leaders, whom he felt were using the war for their own political purposes, caused, in his view, thousands of unnecessary casualties. What comes through very clearly is the Machiavellian turmoil at the highest levels of leadership, and it continues today within the Iranian regime. Under Khomenei, this struggle was encouraged because Khomeini's hold on power depended on keeping the key players off balance and thus controllable. The reader will find himself agreeing with Bani-Sadr on at least one major point: all of this made his role as the elected president of Iran a difficult one indeed. Eventually he felt forced to flee for his life, with further attempts on his life made against him in Paris.

At one point Bani-Sadr writes that "to the very end, the hostage affair—and its counterpart, the alleged arms contracts— would poison the regime. Its repercussions are still a key element in the internal politics of Iran today." There is some merit in this view. And I would add that those same internal politics—the politics of the Iranian revolution—have resulted in a decade of Iranian economic development wasted and much of a generation lost in a senseless and bloody war.

•

FOREWORD

•

This book is vintage Bani-Sadr. It is vintage Iranian. It is a classic example of the Persian penchant for intrigue. Somewhere behind every tree or pillar is the hand of the foreigner, pulling the strings and depriving Iran of its potential. It has always been so. Both in the story it tells, and in the way the story is told, *My Turn to Speak* offers the English-speaking world an important insight into a revolution that profoundly impacted on American interests and may well affect world affairs well into the next century.

AMBASSADOR L. BRUCE LAINGEN

•

PREFACE

On the day of the ceasefire between Iran and Iraq, I recalled Bani-Sadr's answer to a question one of my journalist colleagues had asked him about the ayatollahs' policy. "I am a patriot and I will not comment on the internal situation in Iran until this conflict is resolved." This terrible war was coming to an end, and I immediately telephoned the exiled Iranian president. "I have only one thing to say," he announced. "I can talk now. Let's get started!" Thus, every afternoon in September and October 1988, I interviewed Bani-Sadr and recorded his responses. Each day, we discussed a topic chosen the preceding evening, which he reviewed in the morning with his daughter.

More than fifty cassettes were required for the completion of this work. To give the narrative greater force and make it easier to read, we agreed to omit the questions. Not once did Bani-Sadr become exasperated by my curiosity or my spontaneous remarks. He invariably answered my questions. I wrote down everything he told me, but I edited my notes to a certain extent to emphasize the most important points of our conversations. I hope that this book, unique in both conception and execution, will encourage reflection and will inspire readers to become acquainted with the facts before judging a given event or a given individual.

This book takes us through the doors of a great many places enveloped by deep mystery: Khomeini's homes (in Iran at Qom, and at Neauphle-le-Château in France), the meeting room of the Council of Ministers, military staff headquarters, etc., and shows us the daily political reality of a revolution that has caused a great deal of ink—and even more blood—to flow: the Iranian revolution.

JEAN-CHARLES DENIAU

•

"The freedom of ideas is vital
to truth, but terror kills."
—Rabindranath Tagore

AN EVOLVING REGIME

AT THE VERY OUTSET OF THE REVOLUTION, AS SOON AS Khomeini set foot on Iranian soil, two dangers arose simultaneously: at home, despotism, and abroad, war.

Here in Paris, well before returning to Iran, I began voicing concern about despotism. While we were planning the revolution with Khomeini, I drafted nineteen proposals concerning the form of government we wanted to establish. Two of them dealt with steps to be taken to avoid a possible religious dictatorship dominated by the mullahs. It was on the basis of these nineteen proposals that Khomeini, then residing in Neauphle-le-Château, responded to reporters according to a precisely defined system. First, the reporters wrote down the questions they wanted to ask him, and then a committee—of which I was a member—prepared the answers, which Khomeini repeated verbatim.

For several months Khomeini met with reporters from all over the world. To allay fears, he insisted that the mullahs would not interfere in government affairs. We both committed ourselves to this principle before the entire world.

In Paris, he did not think it possible to overthrow the Shah.

Two or three times a week I reassured him by telling him that the Shah was going to relinquish power. Khomeini was like an exiled chieftain, a pope barred from the Vatican. He was unsure of himself, which is why he repeated whatever he was told. He promised to respect pure Islam, an Islam that teaches, among many other principles, independence, democracy, tolerance, and progress.

The reporters asked Khomeini, "What is your frame of reference? Your model? What is an Islamic state?" We weighed the answers very carefully. To what period in our history could we refer: the Abbasid dynasty? The Umayyads or the first four caliphs? We had to formulate an ideology worthy of a revolution, for we were all convinced that the replacement of one dictatorship with another, even under the banner of Islam, was pointless.

Our work was meticulous and the answers we prepared were carefully thought out. We chose as our reference that period of the Prophet's life when the basic values were founded on the principle of equality among men, which presupposes democratic process and participation by the people in government affairs under a republican system.

These are the Prophet's principles. As soon as we returned to Iran, the first slogan was "Organize councils everywhere."

Clearly, Khomeini broke his promise. Later he would say, "In Paris, I found it expedient to say certain things. In Iran, I find it expedient to refute what I said, and I do so unreservedly."

Nevertheless, it was by espousing freedom that he inspired the revolution.

In Tehran, a very strong movement favoring dictatorship by the mullahs soon took shape. Thus, all of the factors were present for the rapid outbreak of an internal war. I was not a fatalist, however, and I thought that it could be avoided.

A schism developed among the leaders of the new regime. On the one hand were those whose tacit objective was to reestablish despotism, and on the other were those, including myself, who opposed any such outcome.

For a long time, no one wanted to talk about external war, especially not the mullahs. Whenever this danger was mentioned, they accused us of wanting to divert public opinion. For them, all of our problems were internal. Just a few months before the Iraqi assault (in September 1980), when I gave Khomeini information about the troop concentrations, he told me that the military was exaggerating things to prevent the mullahs from gaining control of the army.

Thus, there were three conflicting viewpoints: ours, which held that the threat of war was real; that of the mullahs, who totally denied it; and that of the leftists, for whom war was a necessity. Revolution without war was inconceivable, but the Left only anticipated a civil war that would serve as a means of progressing—as in Russia in 1917—from the first revolution to a second.

It quickly became obvious that the establishment of Islamic power would not be easy. The people would first have to be persuaded to forget the revolutionary ideals that had moved them to action.

It was here that Khomeini's role became important. How could the principles espoused in Paris be replaced with those of Islamic power? He looked for a scapegoat, a satan, and found it in the United States. Beginning with the hostage affair, the "Great Satan" was an effective tool for breaking all forms of resistance to the rise of new powers.

For Khomeini, discrediting the intellectuals was no problem since most of them had ties to the United States. Next, he began a war of attrition against the professionals and the mullahs. Khomeini's men were dispatched with clubs to beat recalcitrant mullahs. Some were even brought to Qom under house arrest. Terrorism was instituted in all its forms: assassinations, public executions, intimidation. Armed opposition groups were no longer a bad thing: they justified the use of violence. At this point we entered the era of provocations, and it was in this way that the driving forces of the mullahs' power were unleashed. A glaring contradiction existed, therefore, between the consciousness of the people, which had been heightened by the revolution, and the backward objectives of religious leaders greedy for absolute power.

The only way to avoid these dangers was to educate the public. I therefore organized meetings and even university courses where I explained to hundreds of participants the principles that had inspired the revolution: liberty, independence, and democracy.

We formed research groups comprising a total of 3,000 academicians to study social problems. Everything later achieved in Iran in the economic sector was conceived during this period, although our resources were limited because we were few in number. We did not have the experienced professionals needed to found a democracy, which explains in part the dictatorship of the mullahs. The people were with us, but we had only a very small minority of the intellectuals on our side because the Marxists shared the same totalitarian views as the mullahs. Today, certain Marxists advocate freedom, but at the time, such was not the case. As for the royalists, a certain number were able to make the transition from one dictatorship to the other with perfect ease.

On both sides, then, groups were forming. Within two months of our arrival in Iran, I met with leftist intellectuals and liberals to make the following plea: "Forget these absurd ideas about a second revolution. Power cannot be the sole aim of the struggle. That is a backward Marxist notion. Freedom must be the goal. Let's work together to build a free society and leave the rest to the following generation. We have fought a revolution; we are going to make it work. Let others carry it forward. A single generation cannot create utopia."

Only two intellectuals reacted favorably; one has since gone over to the totalitarians and the other was in prison (and is now free). Everyone else thought that without professionals, the mullahs could not govern. Everyone was misled by the position of the Tudeh (Communist) Party, which was that the mullahs would initiate a process of development and would therefore need professionals. No one thought for a moment that the mullahs would utterly scorn development, but since the ultimate aim of their existence is martyrdom, they had no use for technicians, academicians, or intellectuals. They were completely insensitive to the concept of a brain drain. One day, Khomeini said, "To hell with intellectuals; we don't need you. Get out!"

Get out, we don't need to build dams, factories, hospitals, or schools because the goal of the regime is actually to teach people how to die. For that, all we need to do is to organize violence.

•

A STRANGE FORM OF ISLAM

To understand the mentality of the mullahs, it is important to realize that their teaching draws inspiration from the philosophy of Aristotle and Plato, as well as the Catholic scholasticism of the Middle Ages. This is the very foundation of their teaching, except for the young mullahs who supported me and whose views concerning freedom and progress often frightened Khomeini. They signed petitions asking me to free them from the hold of those mullahs who were teaching anti-Islamic principles. They wanted to study the Koran from a different perspective, with new teachers. They believed, as I did, that Islam is the key to freeing oneself from the burden of power, whereas the official religious teaching focuses primarily on the difference between good power and evil power. Khomeini, Rafsanjani, and the others were caught up in backward thinking, founded—among other things— on a form of predestination that justifies totalitarianism.

The takeover of the U.S. embassy was wholly in line with Khomeini's strategy of focusing hostility abroad. He attributed such importance to the event that he described it as a second revolution, more important than the first. How can anyone be expected to believe that the takeover of an embassy is more important than a revolution that roused an entire nation? Khomeini knew that by proceeding in this manner he provided himself a field of action previously unimaginable. It was at this moment that the idea of a religious state became viable. He also realized that he could now silence people at will, by threatening them with the accusation of being pro-American. His task was made easier by the compromising documents found in the U.S. embassy. Rumor had it that a great many officials were mentioned. It was true. The regime assembled the documents into over sixty volumes, but by some strange coincidence forgot to publish some of them! This atmosphere made it possible to justify the use of violence against our own people.

Propaganda endlessly repeated that our society—the victim of two centuries of domination by a corrupt West whose only contribution was negative values, debauchery, and sexual depravity—could not integrate Islamic values without a crisis. Why, then, fear a crisis? On the contrary, a crisis was necessary not only in Iran but throughout the world, if possible.

If Iran were consumed in the process, too bad. The important thing was that the necessary conditions could be created for establishing Islam throughout the region.

For the idle young, the Islam of the heart—the spiritual, humanistic Islam—was becoming the militant, violent, material-istic Islam. The revolution, formerly an intellectual objective, was now being fought with guns and clubs. The regime therefore found it necessary to adapt its ideology to this new process.

At this point, the discourse became completely ambiguous. The mullahs nevertheless claimed that this was the same Islam as that preached by Khomeini in Paris. The fact that he never gave a precise definition of Islam is significant. In the pre-revolutionary period, before the Shah's overthrow, everyone knew what Khomeini's version of Islam was. Afterward, this perception was lost in a haze of vague, mutable concepts. The ambiguity of these concepts reveals the state of the regime and its evolution. During the war, for example, as soon as they lost all hope of victory, the mullahs' discourse became increasingly equivocal. It was im-possible to tell whether they were leaning toward peace or escalation of the war. The same was true of Islam, but the crisis concept made it possible to deceive part of the population. Reading all of the statements made between the takeover of the embassy and the beginning of the Iran-Iraq war reveals that two ideological trends were colliding, one attempting to clarify the Koran and the other to obscure it.

These two ideological trends were brought into sharp focus by the subject of exporting the revolution. I envision exporting the revolution as a model, a reference to a humanistic Islam that other Muslim countries can take as an example. The mullahs are wholly opposed to this idea. Exporting the revolution is for them an ideal means of inciting war. They have been more successful than I. The reason is simple: history reveals that for our people—despised and enslaved for centuries by other cultures—the day of retribution has finally arrived. To seize one's own destiny, to assure the material and intellectual development of society, requires much time and involves many uncertainties. Force, on the other hand, is all that is required to impose one's rule on others. These slogans of all-out war and exporting the revolution originated with the Islamic Republic Party, which became the power base of the regime. It also created committees and a host of so-called revolutionary organizations to oversee the struggle in the cities. Most of them were created at the mullahs' initiative under the Mehdi Bazargan government. Bazargan, however, categorically rejected export of the revolution and structural change. It seems that for the first head of the government of the Islamic Republic, appointed by Khomeini, the revolution was already too much.

By all-out war, the mullahs meant holy war, *jihad*. This is another major topic of controversy among the mullahs. They discussed holy war as though Islam permitted the waging of war to liberate others. They made a pretense of forgetting that, for Shiites, war is prohibited until the twelfth *Imam*, who is hidden, returns to the world. In his absence, no Muslim people can initiate a war of aggression; they can only undertake defensive actions.

I have had many discussions on this subject with the mullahs. I said that the Koran forbids the use of violence to force an idea on others; it is explicit on this subject. The Prophet never took the initiative in any war. The problem is that all revolutions begin or end with a bloodbath. It is inconceivable, however, that the Prophet would not have found a way out of this dilemma. Thus, the Koran teaches how to prevent non-believers from starting a war and, if the believer is unable to prevent it, how to ensure that it will not last.

Many mullahs are not familiar with the study of the Koran as a "method," which is the literal translation of the word. They are unaware of the Prophet's recommendations because, strangely, seminaries are not founded on the Koran itself, but on tradition and on what is said *about* the holy book.

We often discussed the problem of holy war in the Revolutionary Council with Khomeini. One day, in his son's presence, I laughed and told him, "You are too fond of force!" He responded, "Of course, it's necessary. With your theory of non-violence, it's impossible to solve serious problems." These private remarks did not count; what did matter was his public justification of violence. He always said the same thing: "What Bani-Sadr says is excellent, but only for the long term. Right now, we don't have time to preach non-violence."

The precepts of the Prophet do not teach us to seek sacrifice and death; on the contrary, they tell us how to avoid subjugation, how to live freely, independently, and with respect. Force is the ultimate weapon, a sort of medicine to be used only when others try to overpower you. I told Khomeini repeatedly, "You believe in force, not resistance. When you have force, you use it to destroy. But if another is stronger than you, you submit."

In this area we scored some points because the young people quickly realized that the theory of force was going to plunge the country into darkness. Had there been no war, we would have been totally victorious. Even with Khomeini, the mullahs would not have been able to impose their dictatorship.

The mullahs had access to the radio, the newspapers, and the Friday prayers. We had to do without all of that. We had only one newspaper, *Enghelab Eslami*, and yet, as far as public opinion is concerned, we routed them. The proof is that the mullahs had to organize a coup to get rid of me. With public opinion on their side, they would not have found it necessary to repress my supporters as they did after my departure.

As soon as tensions with our neighbor Iraq developed, the concept of export of the revolution was changed to export of the crisis. It was no longer enough simply to change other nations by involving our revolutionaries in their struggle; we had to impose our crisis on them, along with its corollaries of terrorism, hostage-taking, and so on.

A SOCIETY UNDER GUARDIANSHIP

Ali Akbar Rafsanjani, Mohammad Husseni Beheshti, and Khomeini formulated two political theories anticipating their seizure of power. First, regarding the mullahs, they recommended an organization modeled on that of the Catholic church. A pope, cardinals, and bishops were needed. In Iran, we did not have a hierarchy, properly speaking.

Regarding the administration of the new regime, their theory recommended eliminating everything left over from the days of the Shah. They proposed structural changes designed to prevent a coup d'état such as the one organized against Mohammad Mossadegh. They wanted to create vigilance committees composed of three individuals: a Revolutionary Guard, a member of the revolutionary tribunals, and a member of the revolutionary committees (the mullahs' police force). The objective, among other things, was first to dominate the army, then disband it and replace it with the Revolutionary Guards. To introduce their plan, they used documents found in the U.S. embassy describing the means of subverting the revolution by inciting an internal war, sparked by an army-backed tribal uprising and strikes in the cities, the universities, and anywhere the ground was favorable, especially in Kurdistan.

I was friends with Ayatollah Taleghani, the most prominent religious leader of Tehran, whom I had known for a long time since he had been in prison with my father in the days of Reza Shah Pahlavi. We were always quite frank with one another. We both realized that a very powerful movement was forming in favor of dictatorship, and I suggested that he join me in resisting it. We spent two days in Qom at the home of a mutual friend discussing the coming dangers, which he perceived as clearly as I did. He repeatedly asked, "How can we say to the people that their Guide, the one they have claimed for a quarter of a century, has two faces: the one they know, and another, the face of a dictator?" We agreed that it was possible to create obstacles to dictatorship without directly confronting Khomeini. And yet, it was this same Taleghani who proposed the creation of the Assembly of Experts, an initiative that Khomeini immediately approved and that was a decisive step in the establishment of the mullahs' power.

I was elected to this Assembly of Experts—which was in fact a constituent assembly (74 members, one for every 500,000 citizens) convened in the summer of 1979—with the second largest number of votes in Tehran, behind Taleghani but well ahead of Ayatollah Montazeri.

In the proceedings of this assembly—ultimately comprised almost exclusively of clerics, despite the fact that it was originally to have included only a minority—Taleghani supported my opposition to the power movement, but without committing himself directly. Thus, I had to act alone, or nearly so, since he did side with me on a crucial article of the Constitution: the sovereignty of the Islamic jurist.* At issue was the question of whether spiritual matters took precedence over temporal matters. Like me, Taleghani was fiercely opposed to this principle. We therefore decided to resist by publishing articles warning the public about this law, which would lead straight to religious fascism, and by waging a public attack based on historical research. We showed that 90 percent of the foremost Shiite religious leaders were opposed to the sovereignty of the Islamic jurist. Even Khomeini opposed it in Paris. For us, the authors of these constitutional articles were suspect because of their foreign connections. In the Mossadegh era, for example, they had close ties with the British and the Americans. Our hostility was not merely theoretical.

They even went so far as to introduce an amendment giving sixteen powers to the *faqib* (doctor of theology authorized to give opinions on Koranic laws), ranging from space to nature and including animals and property. In short, the "Guide of the Revolution" had absolute power over everything that moved on earth. What an aberration! Not all of the members of the assembly were clerics, however. Closely associated with Montazeri were laymen such as Hassan Ayyat, who, during the Shah's reign had led a dissolute life. He had close ties to one of the factions of Mossadegh's National Front before participating in the coup organized by the CIA to overthrow it. This same Hassan Ayyat also served as a contact between the Americans and the followers of Abolghassam Kashani, the most prominent cleric at the time. Our distrust was justified.

We did everything we could to stop the passage of this article of law on the sovereignty of the Islamic jurist. I was one of the seven members of a committee appointed to discuss this specific article of the future constitution. Our task was to determine whether national interest or the law should prevail. If it is acknowledged that Islamic law is paramount, the sovereignty of

---

* The most learned religious leader, the one with the most extensive knowledge in matters of justice, theology, and so on.

the Islamic jurist justifies religious power. A problem arises immediately in this case. How can a religious jurist understand the economic, political, and military interests of the country? The mullahs could not answer these questions and therefore refused an open, public debate on this subject, preferring instead to insist, without explanation, that national interest and the law are indissociable.

Our strategy of creating an atmosphere extremely hostile to the proposed amendment outside the Assembly was successful, for they did not dare give full executive power to Khomeini as *faqih*. According to Article 110 of the Constitution, he is commander in chief of the armed forces, but his power is limited to appointing the chiefs of staff and commanders of the army, the air force, and the navy, upon the proposal of the Defense Council. The actual command is held by the president of the republic. It could be said that all of the government acts accomplished by Khomeini were illegal since, according to the letter of the law, he had no executive power.

The Islamic Republic Party was hostile to me from that moment on. Previously, it was not opposed to my candidacy for the presidency of the republic. It even encouraged and supported me.

This triumph over the sovereignty of the Islamic jurist had its price: the mullahs took their revenge by stripping the office of president of all real political power. They knew that I had every chance of being elected, so they acted accordingly. The president had the honors, but not the power. He could appoint ministers, but he could not dismiss them. These power struggles went on inside the regime without anyone on the outside being aware of them.

Knowing that the powers of the new president would be limited, I was reluctant to run. The prospect of working with only a fragment of power did not interest me. My advisers encouraged me, however, because the important thing then was to further the principles of the revolution during the campaign. This is what I did in meetings, speeches, and newspaper articles. I staunchly defended independence, democracy, progress, and an Islam compatible with these three essential values of our revolution. The results were consistent with my efforts since I was elected

•

with 76 percent of the vote. Clearly, a majority of the people were opposed to government by the mullahs.

Khomeini made the best of it, but his distrust of me only increased. His fears are illustrated by the following anecdote. My swearing-in ceremony was held in the hospital, where Khomeini was very ill at the time. We were in his room. I kissed his hand like a son, because my sympathy was both genuine and deep, but it did not prevent me from saying that I had been elected by the people and that I represented their sovereignty. This statement of course displeased him because, for him, only the Islamic jurist was sovereign. That evening, when the ceremony was broadcast on television, I noticed that no one could hear what I had said. I knew that he had given orders to that effect. Even when he was sick and near death—as we all believed, including himself—he was still at work.

The mullahs realized that they were not going to win this way, especially since Khomeini was sick, so they went to see him. He told them, quite simply, that the way to oppose me was to take control of parliament. This would be difficult without resorting to fraud since the people, by electing me, had just signified their rejection of the mullahs.

The mullahs were not above rigging the elections, however, and so won a majority in the National Assembly. A committee to oversee the election, appointed by the Revolutionary Council, an organization otherwise devoted to the mullahs, nevertheless observed many irregularities. Khomeini took no notice of this and declared the election valid. My mistake was to give in to him on this point. A fatal mistake.

The process of seizing power entered a new phase when the mullahs decided to ban the National Front and several newspapers. This was necessary, they said, because the party and the newspapers were counterrevolutionary. Their logic also indicated the necessity of weakening the president. For this, they devised a theory. "The Iranian people have become accustomed to the idea of a shah, a political leader. With the shah deposed, the person who symbolizes this shah is Bani-Sadr. It will therefore be necessary to change presidents several times to dispel the awe attached to this office."

According to Shahpour Bakhtiar, the Shah's last prime

minister, then in exile in Paris, "Bani-Sadr is dangerous because he is a capable individual; if he remains in office, all chances of a restoration will be lost. If he is ousted, we will benefit because the mullahs, who are uneducated and incapable of governing, will also be overthrown."

I think that this statement of Bakhtiar's also expressed the wishes of the superpowers, especially the United States. At the time, the idea of a democracy in Iran, in an oil-producing region, was not at all to their liking. The proof is that dictatorships were established at that time in two neighboring countries, Turkey and Pakistan, both of which were allies of the Shah and friendly with the Americans.

THE SPECTER OF A RESTORATION

The threat of a restoration, of a return of the old regime, frightened everyone. Sadegh Ghotbzadeh had purchased a document in Paris for $200,000 that described a royalist plan to regain power with Iraq's help. It was later confirmed that this plan, purchased from a South American, had been formulated in a hotel on the Boulevard Raspail by a group of Israeli generals, Americans, and exiled Iranians. It called for destroying the regime by means of an external war. To get to the bottom of this, I asked our air force to see if there were any troop concentrations in the areas mentioned in the plan. As it turned out, there were—but they were not royalists, they were Iraqis. This confirmed the information obtained by the intelligence section of the Iranian Army that the Iraqis, with U.S. approval, were planning to attack. This plan also mentioned a meeting in Jordan between Zbigniew Brzezinski, President Jimmy Carter's national security adviser, and Saddam Hussein, two months before the Iraqi attack. There was nothing surprising in this since Iraq could never have attacked without a green light from the Americans and the Soviets. The plan also detailed the military preparations and the attack zones, which would later become the front. In the western region of the country we had four armored divisions, two non-armored divisions, and three air bases, which the organizers of the plan wanted to weaken or neutralize. This operation, called "Nojet," consisted

•

of organizing cells of officers and noncommissioned officers in the armored divisions, who, when the time came, would join the aggressors. Four of the eight plots we uncovered in the army were organized in these four divisions. The others were planned in backup divisions. Knowledge of this plan contributed to the army's disorganization because it led to wide-scale intervention by the mullahs.

When the Iraqis invaded Iran, 270 officers and noncommissioned officers from the Khuzestan divisions were in prison. Not all of them were subversives; far from it—there were no more than twenty or thirty in all—but this was the chance to be rid of the army. At the time, the mullahs did not believe in the war. They thought that no one could attack revolutionary Iran because of its prestige in the world.

But this was not all. To completely neutralize the army, the plan called for uprisings and a war in Kurdistan. Very recently, Gassemlou's party, the PDKI, published a document claiming that a rival organization, the pro-Communist Komoleh, started the war in Kurdistan. The truth is that this war was linked to the Iraqi assault.

The failure to neutralize the army was due to the fact that the interception of this plan enabled us very quickly to crush these plots as well as the Kurdish revolt. The Iraqis thought that we could use only 20 percent of our air power; as it turned out, we were able to use 90 percent.

The plots, the Kurdish uprising, and the disturbances in the cities were not chance events. Our ambassador to the Soviet Union, Mohammad Mockri, sent me a document one day that was an exact duplicate of the invasion plan purchased by Ghotbzadeh. According to Mockri, the document had been given to him by some French friends in the CNRS (Centre National de Recherche Scientifique, or National Center for Scientific Research) where he once worked as a researcher. I thought this very strange. A short time later, the Soviet ambassador came to see me. He was an affable, courteous man with whom one could talk. I asked him if it was not he who had accidentally communicated the plan to our ambassador. He laughed and said nothing. Strangely, Mockri is now in prison in Iran for spying for the Soviets. He was denounced by a KGB agent who had worked in Iran before going

•

over to the British. This episode proved that the plan purchased by Ghotbzadeh was not concocted by some crook to make money. It was a genuine counterrevolutionary plan.

We eventually solved these internal problems: Kurdistan, Khuzestan, and West Azerbaijan, where a group was regularly sabotaging the railroad.

Although the situation in various parts of the country was stabilizing, the regime itself was in turmoil. Citing the disturbances in the provinces, the plots in the army, and the demonstrations in the cities, Beheshti introduced a plan while I was away entitled "Measures to Prevent a Coup d'état." In it, reference was made to the Mossadegh experience, which had shown that unless action is taken quickly counterrevolutionaries take control of the situation. This was not incorrect, but it is nevertheless important to understand what is meant by "counterrevolutionary." As far as the lower-level professionals, the popular masses, the police agents, and the soldiers were concerned, this policy was effective because it inspired fear. The theory of the mullahs could be summed up in one sentence: "If you fail to intimidate others, expect to be eliminated." Each Guard knew that if "others" won, he would be executed. It was therefore his duty to sow terror as a preventive measure.

Beheshti's plan called for the formation of a committee composed of three individuals: a militant from the urban revolutionary committee, a Revolutionary Guard, and a member of the revolutionary tribunals. Under the direction of the Revolutionary Council, this committee would take charge of the country. The military leaders and all of the officials of the old regime would be arrested. First, the committee would take control of all the country's political institutions and organize a severe repression of opponents of the Islamic Republic. Second, the army would be dissolved and replaced by the Revolutionary Guards. The Revolutionary Council had approved the plan. As it was being discussed, Bazargan protested, "This plan is political assassination for Bani-Sadr; at least wait until he is here to carry it out."

This plan was merely a modification of the one described by William H. Sullivan, the last U.S. ambassador to Iran. In his book, *Mission to Iran*, published in 1981, Sullivan tells how he, Bazargan, and Mousavi Ardebili, Khomeini's representative, had agreed in

•

January 1979 to establish a stable regime in Iran, based on an alliance between the clerics and the army.

Beheshti's plan only substituted the Guards for the army because the clerics insisted on governing with their own army. Beheshti repeated at every opportunity, "This is not our army; we must have our own military organization."

Along with other members of the Council, I opposed this plan, which, in the end, was scrapped. I now believe that the coup against me, and everything that followed, was simply the execution of this plan, the origin of which goes back to the agreement with Sullivan.

According to the Americans, the Pahlavi regime was unstable because it was supported only by the army, every other force in the country being hostile to it. The army and the clerics, on the other hand, could create the foundation for a solid regime.

Early in the summer of 1980, the threat of a creeping coup d'état and an external war became more compelling than ever when I received another report from the second army bureau confirming the Iraqi plan of attack approved by the Americans. When I received this report, I wrote on the cover in red letters, "Go explain this to Khomeini." The military did go to him, and a few days later I met with the Imam to ask his opinion. Again, he was implacable. "The soldiers do not want the clerics checking up on them. They write these reports saying there is a threat of war merely to escape our control. No one would dare attack Iran."

Why was he so sure that no one would attack Iran? It could not have been intuition on his part; someone must have given him assurances. Who else but the Americans had an interest in lulling him into a false sense of security? After war was declared, Khomeini told Montazeri, "I never saw this second bureau report." What a lie!

A PRESIDENT UNDER SURVEILLANCE

Another step toward clerical despotism was taken as soon as the government was formed. After my election, Khomeini, reassured about the state of his health, realized that a popular president would overshadow him. Since this would be an intolerable

•

situation for him, he decided to appoint a prime minister antagonistic toward me. This was part of his method of dominating others through contradictions and divisions. The most important thing for him was that the prime minister not agree with the president.

A considerable obstacle arose immediately because the Constitution specifies that the president of the Republic and the parliament must jointly approve the appointment of the prime minister. In theory, then, parliament did not have the power to force anyone on me. The intention of the authors of the Constitution was to divide the responsibility for this appointment while at the same time limit the power of the president, who cannot dismiss the prime minister once he is appointed.

I knew that the Islamic Republic Party had voted to nominate its own candidate. The purpose of this vote was to derail any candidates in the party who might have supported me. Ali Rajai, Beheshti's man, was elected by 40 votes, even though he was never registered in the party. To impose their favorite on me, they asked Khomeini to publish a document stating that the appointment of the prime minister is a religious obligation requiring the Imam's approval. Khomeini did not dare go so far as that, but it did not stop him from working against me. He sent his son Ahmed to Karim Sanjabi, president of the National Front and now in exile in the United States, to offer him the post of prime minister on the condition that he oppose the president. Sanjabi refused. Khomeini originally proposed Ahmad Madani to head the government. I rejected him because I did not think he was qualified. This and several other proposals lead me to believe that Khomeini was not in league with Beheshti, unless he knew in advance that I would refuse and wanted to force me to accept the mullahs' candidate, Rajai, as a last resort.

Khomeini knew full well that Rajai was incapable of governing Iran. That was not the problem; Rajai's apparent opposition to the president was enough for the mullahs to shove him to the front. Here again, there was a slight difference between reality and appearances. I nicknamed Rajai "dead brain." Khomeini's son-in-law remarked to the Ayatollah one day, "Bani-Sadr says that Rajai is a 'dead brain,' but I spoke with him and I found that he has no brain at all." Rajai was undoubtedly the tool

Beheshti was looking for to implement his plan. Through him, the revolutionary organizations planned to seize control and sweep aside all obstacles blocking their path to power. I could not state publicly that Rajai was the puppet of these organizations because that would have played into their hands. They would have immediately retorted, "Look, Bani-Sadr, president of the Republic, is against the revolutionary organizations." Any such denunciation would only have increased the hostility of these organizations toward me. I decided to make the best of it and to work with Rajai, who was merely the committee's drive belt installed by Beheshti, Rafsanjani, and the others.

I have a large volume of correspondence dating from this period. Khomeini, Rajai, parliament, and I wrote many letters to each other. Never, except when I wrote to Khomeini, did I ever mention the position of Rajai, the mullahs' puppet.

I tried to make this poor, manipulated prime minister understand that he would be one of the first victims of the mullahs' totalitarian power. And so he was; he was killed in a bombing. I also told Beheshti, the architect of the plan, "You will be eliminated before I am because you're not an important cleric, you're not a prominent intellectual, you're not in the military—and yet, you want to take the leading role. Impossible! You use others, but you are also used, and you will be eliminated." This is precisely what happened.

My advisers told me to accept this cohabitation with Rajai. Bazargan was of the same opinion. "Leave them alone; they'll hold out for two, three months—no more; then they'll give up." I knew that the mullahs' tactic of governing through an intermediary would continue for a much longer period, but I acquiesced because I sensed that war was approaching and I did not want to air our power struggles in public.

Khomeini sent Mousavi Ardebili to my home to ask me to let the government do its job and to focus my attention on the army. I expressed disagreement, despite the insistence of Khomeini, who told parliament, "Do not approve any ministers nominated by the president unless they are maktabis," that is, hard-liners. I was furious because, for the first time, he was interfering with the prerogatives of the president. Clearly, he wanted to neutralize me. I went to see him and he insisted that I work with these men as he had told me to do. I shouted loud enough for everyone in his neighborhood in Jamoram to hear, "You betray yourself. You are not keeping the promises you made in Paris. You do not respect the Constitution you yourself approved. I warned you the day I submitted my candidacy for the presidency. You should never have approved these elections because you have no respect for the law. Moreover, you are going to give in to the Americans, which is totally unacceptable because you played a vital role in the revolution, unlike Beheshti, Rafsanjani, and the others, who did nothing. They grafted themselves onto the revolution with your help, you who fought for twenty-five years by preaching a humanistic philosophy of Islam before betraying everyone and embracing the worst interpretation of the Koran, that which exalts martyrdom, death, and ignorance."

Throughout this tirade he kept saying, "Hurry up! You have a ceremony to attend in Kashan, and they are waiting for you." He wanted me to leave. He even had the nerve to tell me that I had personally chosen Rajai. I exploded, "How can you lie about that? You forget that you forced that incompetent on me." He changed tack by saying that a mullah had told him that I had accepted Rajai in a working meeting, before he was forced on me. He said, and I quote, "I believe what this mullah told me; you, I do not believe."

I shouted, "I was elected by the people; you have known me for over fifteen years; and you have more confidence in an insignificant mullah!"

On returning from Kashan, I summoned the mullah in question, and I recorded our conversation. He admitted having lied and asked me to forgive him. I sent the tape to Khomeini, together with a long letter.

In any case, Khomeini's mind was made up, which enabled the government, at the mullahs' instigation, to set a goal from which it never deviated for a second, despite the war: the elimination of both me and the army.

Two weeks before the Iraqi attack, I threatened Khomeini with public exposure of the mullahs' plan to take over the government if Beheshti, Rafsanjani, and the others did not stop their scheming. I wanted to take advantage of the commemoration of Black Friday—September 8, 1978, the date the Shah's regime massacred a crowd of demonstrators in Tehran—to create a scandal. To counter this threat, they issued a warning over the radio that a violent attack might occur during the ceremony. The Guards wanted me to find myself facing an empty square. I asked the manager of the radio station to broadcast an announcement denying these rumors of an attack and inviting the people to gather in Freedom Square. The announcement, read every fifteen minutes, was definitely heard because the people responded en masse to my appeal.

Khomeini immediately sent his son to me with a warning: "Be careful of what you say. We don't want a crisis." I decided not to create a scandal after all, but I did punctuate my speech with enough innuendos to make the mullahs understand me. Their reaction was instantaneous. They denounced my remarks with such vehemence that everyone knew I had touched a nerve, Khomeini most of all. He later reproached me severely for this speech. It became obvious at once that the size of the demonstration had frightened him.

Two days later, at a ceremony to commemorate the anniversary of Taleghani's death, Khomeini's son-in-law Eshraghi tried to pacify me. He explained that Khomeini was worried because he had never before seen a layman attract a larger crowd than the mullahs could. It was inconceivable to the Imam that a layman could mobilize an entire city, as I had. Something had to be done.

I realized that the internal conflict was going to intensify. Meanwhile, we should have been marshaling our forces because the Iraqi attack was becoming more of a reality every day.

REAGAN AND KHOMEINI

The Agreement

AFTER THE FALL OF THE BAZARGAN GOVERNMENT ON November 6, 1979, I accepted the post of minister of foreign affairs. It was my first executive position since returning to Iran. My first priority was to solve the hostage problem to prevent it from becoming the pretext for a war of restoration. I was convinced that falling into the trap of hostility would open the door to counterrevolutionary action. Also, when the Revolutionary Council suggested that I take charge of this ministry, I immediately asked what was to be done with the hostages. I went to see the students occupying the U.S. embassy and told them, quite frankly, what I thought. "You think that you have taken America hostage. What a delusion! In fact, you have made Iran the hostage of the Americans."

The next day, in an article in *Enghelab Eslami*, I strongly criticized the attitude of the students, who would listen to nothing, and then I went to see Khomeini in Qom to find out what he thought about it. He could not have been more explicit: "They are not diplomats, but spies; they are being watched." Initially, however, the plan was to lock them up for a few days and then release them. In fact, the reason the hostages were taken was to get rid of Bazargan. Khomeini, who had chosen Bazargan himself, could not change his mind so soon after installing him. It was therefore necessary to find some indirect approach to depose Bazargan, and the embassy affair was the ideal pretext for getting rid of him by accusing him of being in sympathy with the United States. I should mention that I contacted Bazargan at the time and advised him not to resign. Nevertheless, we were not on good terms. He was surprised by the step I took. We saw each other later, and I asked him, "Why did you put yourself in that impossible situation with the Americans?" He answered, "The hostage-taking was nothing but a ploy to get rid of me, but I didn't realize it right away."

Ordinarily, I would have known who had decided to take the hostages because the students "of the Imam's line" were subject to a five-member council—of which I was a member, together with Hassan Habibi, the current vice president; Khamenei; Mousavi Khoeiniha; and Shabestari, a cleric—and we certainly never contemplated any such action. Moreover, three of the five members—Mohammad Shabestari, Habibi, and I—never officially knew who organized this operation using the Revolutionary Guards as a cover. In fact, the decision to take the Americans hostage came from Khomeini's entourage, supported by certain members of the Islamic Republic Party. They wanted to use the hostages to create a climate favorable to their takeover of the government. It is inconceivable that the Guards would have taken such a step alone.

From the beginning, the hostage affair was handled illogically. When one is preparing for an enemy attack or has decided to conduct an internal policy of confrontation, care must be taken to provide the necessary means. How was it that Khomeini and his aides planned the embassy takeover without considering the internal, regional, and international contexts? They exhibited a rare lack of foresight by doing nothing to protect our resources or our money and by failing to import the spare parts already paid for and stockpiled at American airports first. There was no hurry. These basic precautions could have been taken and then, afterward, the embassy could have been seized to obtain the Shah's extradition. One did not have to be an expert to see that the hostage affair was going to paralyze us economically. Early in the revolution, Ibrahim Yazdi received a report from the United States calling for a blockade of Iran. When I arrived at the foreign affairs ministry, I found two very explicit memorandums on this subject.

Thus, we knew what was in store for us, yet no one did anything about it. Everything that happened as a result of the hostage affair occurred with the full knowledge of the Iranian authorities. Our spare parts and our funds were frozen in the United States. A child could have spotted the trap. We found a document in the U.S. embassy in Tehran outlining a plan to freeze Iranian funds. This plan, which predates the hostage affair, was developed by Chase Manhattan Bank, which feared that revolutionary Iran would not pay its debts. It sent experts to Iran to investigate the regime. Their report concluded that there was no government, no justice, and therefore no law in Iran. Since government by the mullahs was synonymous with anarchy, the U.S. courts could be petitioned to freeze Iranian funds. This initial maneuver failed because proving to a court that Iran was a lawless country was not an easy matter. The international jurists who advised the banks found the plan unworkable. They prepared a second plan that resulted in our funds being frozen by the president of the United States.

What a lack of foresight! Withdrawing our funds should have been our first reprisal against the Americans for harboring the Shah. We could have taken legal action to obtain delivery of our spare parts and, as a last resort, occupied the embassy. In this way, we would have placed ourselves in the best possible position in case of an Iraqi attack.

Apprised of these facts by the Americans, Saddam Hussein knew when he attacked that we lacked spare parts and that the few we had were stored haphazardly in warehouses. During the Shah's reign, the Americans had asked for $250 million to provide computer management of the spare parts inventories they had sold us. The Shah had agreed, but the revolution had prevented completion of the work. Our military depots were in an indescribable mess.

With the approval of the Revolutionary Council and Khomeini,

•

I asked the United Nations Security Council to deal with the hostage problem. We had formulated three demands that I believed were acceptable to the United Nations. Our jurists had worked very hard on this. On November 28, 1979, I was preparing for a flight to New York when, two hours before my departure, I heard on the radio Khomeini's announcement forbidding the presence of any representative of Iran at the United Nations. I immediately met with the members of the Revolutionary Council and asked them to go with me to Qom to see Khomeini. He received us in a severe, distant manner. The mullahs understood. They left immediately, but I did not. I said to him, "You have consulted no one, neither the government nor the Revolutionary Council. Your announcement goes against all of the decisions we have made together. You are going to make Iran look ridiculous in front of the whole world because this meeting of the Security Council was requested by us for the purpose of obtaining extradition of the Shah, the return of his assets, and the formation of a committee to investigate the Americans' dealings in Iran."

The Americans, as can be easily imagined, had done everything they could to prevent this UN meeting. My three advisers—Mansour Farhang, Said Sanjabi, and Ahmad Salamatian—had fought hard to obtain the approval of the required number of Security Council members. We also had the endorsement of UN Secretary General Kurt Waldheim and the nonaligned countries. The media considered this a diplomatic coup and a virtual slap in the face for the United States.

Khomeini, somewhat embarrassed, justified his about-face by saying, "I could not accept the idea of the Security Council condemning Iran in your presence. As far as we were concerned, it would have been your undoing."

"So what?" I replied. "Even if we were condemned, what difference would it make? Every day, the Council condemns a country for one reason or another. Imagine for a moment that we had won, because I believe that our request was justifiable. The Shah, as everyone knows, did not go to the United States for medical attention. His physician lives in Canada, so he could have been cared for somewhere else. He is there for political reasons."

Hearing this, Khomeini said that he had been told the exact opposite.

"Where do you get your information? I am the foreign affairs minister. I am the one you should be asking for explanations."

"Forget it," he replied.

Who gave Khomeini these ideas? That is the question I asked myself immediately. I thought long and hard about Ghotbzadeh, whom I accused of giving the Imam false information. I later realized that, in reality, Khomeini had only one concern: to prevent a layman from gaining prestige in the international arena.

The outcome of this episode? Another failure for Iran.

On returning from Qom, I met with the Revolutionary Council and tendered my resignation, asking Ghotbzadeh to take my place, which he did.

After my election to the presidency of the Republic, the internal atmosphere surrounding the hostage affair became oppressive, especially as a result of two audio tapes made available to me by the Mujahedeen. One was about Beheshti, and the other, Hassan Ayyat. The Beheshti tape was of a private conversation between him and one of his friends. He very distinctly said, "The hostage affair must be used to get rid of Bani-Sadr." I played the tape for Khomeini's son and for Mousavi Ardebili, later president of the Supreme Judicial Council. Beheshti, when asked to explain himself, said that someone had imitated his voice, to which Ahmed Khomeini replied that it was impossible to imitate someone for hours at a time. What surprised me most was that Khomeini, despite this irrefutable evidence, worked against me and not Beheshti.

The other tape was also very clear. Hassan Ayyat said, "Everything we have done—the public disturbances, the demonstrations, the provocations—had only one purpose: to incapacitate the elected president. Unfortunately, he has escaped from the trap each time. But this time, the hostages are the trap and he will need his ancestors' help to get out of this one."

The plans we were making, the composition of parliament—everything—convinced me that war was imminent. I therefore wanted to solve the hostage question as quickly as possible.

•

UNOFFICIAL NEGOTIATIONS

Two French lawyers, François Chéron and Christian Bourguet, had drawn up a draft agreement between Iran and the Carter administration (see box below). This draft had Khomeini's full approval.

At the request of Kurt Waldheim, international judges were to conduct an investigation of the Shah's regime and meet with the hostages. The students of the Imam's line—the Americans' jailers—refused, and Khomeini, instead of encouraging moderation, added fuel to the fire. He issued a statement demanding that they publish the findings of their investigation before being allowed to meet with the hostages.

The judges came to see me. "How can you expect us to agree to this? We have in fact concluded that the Americans collaborated with Iran during the Pahlavi regime and that they are partly responsible for the corruption that existed then, but we cannot publish our findings with this threat hanging over our heads. Our report would be meaningless. Everyone would say that it was written or published under coercion, that it is a trade-off for releasing the hostages. It would be worthless." I agreed with them. I asked them to stay and to wait until I had changed Khomeini's mind. But, instead of listening to me, they left.

A few days later, Khomeini modified his tactics by issuing a statement announcing that the fate of the hostages was henceforth in parliament's hands. For me, this was synonymous with permanent deadlock. The mullahs knew that if this problem were solved, the external threat would vanish and they would find it extremely difficult to seize power. That was the crux of the problem. To justify himself, Khomeini told me, "Iran needs you as president and your prestige must remain intact. The hostage affair is a dirty business; let parliament handle it."

Excerpts from the draft agreement between the Carter administration and the Iranian regime for the release of the hostages in the U.S. embassy in Tehran. This official draft was carried out in part since an investigative committee did go to Tehran.

(Translation.)

Scenario reviewed

I. Principles and Procedures (unchanged from the previous version)

The United States and Iran agree:

1) to accept the principle of the development of a scenario, the initial stages of which will be precisely defined and the following stages defined in detail on the basis of the progress of events;

2) to implement this scenario with the aid of persons approved by both parties.

II. Appointment of a Fact-finding Commission (the changes show in detail the sequence of events in New York time)

1) It is specified in the approval of this scenario that the secretary general of the United Nations will appoint a fact-finding commission "to hear Iranian grievances, to find a solution to the crisis between the United States and Iran as quickly as possible" and that Iran wants this commission to talk with each of the hostages.

....

III. Work of the Commission

1) The commission will not leave New York for Tehran until the above announcement has been made by the United States. It will endeavor to commence its work in Tehran at the beginning of the following week.

2) The commission will hold its meetings in private and will receive evidence and documents submitted to it by the Iranian authorities.

....

IV. Final Stages

1) The transfer of the hostages under the protection of the Iranian government will be made either in a hospital or at the embassy, after the "students" have left the building (Day 1).

2) Return of the commission to New York (Day 1 + 1).

3) Submission to the secretary general of the commission's report, which shall include proceedings and recommendations. Publication of the report in the form of a United Nations document. The report will express the following principle, among others, as a recommendation to all governments:

Governments must respect and guarantee the exercise, within the framework of their internal legislation, of the rights of Iran:

•

a) to institute proceedings against the Shah, his family, or his associates, on the grounds of grave suspicion of criminal acts brought to light in the report.

b) to institute proceedings to recover the assets which, in the report, are presumed to have been illegally removed from Iran by the Shah, his family, or his associates (Day 1 + 2).

4) Release of the hostages and their departure from Iran (Day 1 + 3).

....

6) Formation of a joint commission to resolve outstanding bilateral problems. (On a date to be determined by Iran and the United States within a period of one month following Day 1.)

Consolidating the mullahs' power was not Khomeini's only reason for entrusting the hostage affair to parliament. There was talk within the government of deals being made prior to the American elections. I have proof of contacts between Khomeini and the supporters of Ronald Reagan as early as the spring of 1980.

Khomeini's justification of a "no show" was the end result of these contacts, the sole purpose of which was to handicap Carter's re-election bid by preventing the hostages' release before the American elections in November 1980. Rafsanjani, Beheshti, and Ahmed Khomeini played a key role in proposing this agreement to the Reagan team. I did everything I could to change Khomeini's mind, but I failed.

In early July, a Frenchman introducing himself as a representative of Valéry Giscard d'Estaing met with me. I complained about European and French policy toward Iran. His response shocked me. "President Giscard d'Estaing would like very much to intervene, but the Americans have given him to understand that they are ready to go to war over two countries: Iran and Germany. 'If you take one step toward Iran,' they told him, 'we will break your legs.'"

Also in the spring of 1980, Khomeini's nephew residing in Spain was contacted by some Americans close to Reagan. They proposed an agreement: not a reconciliation between governments but a secret agreement between leaders. He came to see me and told me that the Americans wanted to establish secret relations with me, and that if I refused, they would make the same offer to Beheshti and Rafsanjani. I categorically refused to become involved in any such scheme. I have never mentioned this until now, because I did not want to cause trouble for this Iranian.

It is no coincidence that everyone who agreed to deal with the Americans—Beheshti, Rafsanjani, Behzad Nabavi, Moshen Rezai—later held important positions in the regime. Except for Beheshti, who was assassinated, they all survived their swindling and their numerous betrayals. After my departure, Moshen Rezai became commander in chief of the Revolutionary Guards, a position he still held in 1990. It is no coincidence either that their names were all mentioned in connection with Irangate.

On August 20, I attended a meeting at the home of Mahdavi-Khani, a member of the Revolutionary Council. I again mentioned the hostage problem, the need for spare parts, and the imminent possibility of an Iraqi assault. I repeatedly insisted that a rapid solution of the hostage problem would result in the lifting of the blockade and would help us in our preparations for the war, which I said was close at hand. Beheshti then interrupted, "If we solve the hostage problem, you must not criticize us!"

I answered, "Why would I do that if you are working in Iran's interest?"

He then handed me a sheet of paper. "Write it down; promise that you will not criticize us."

I found the procedure extremely odd, but nothing more.

Two weeks after that meeting, on September 3, the ambassador of the Federal Republic of Germany handed me an offer from Jimmy Carter, which to me seemed very favorable. I thought again of the Beheshti incident. It could not be the same thing since this offer was strictly official. For what other reason, then, did he want me to promise not to criticize him? I realized that there was another agreement in the works and that it had nothing to do with Carter. With whom, then, if not his rival for the White House, Ronald Reagan? Beheshti, the instigator of the agreement, wanted to protect himself by making sure that I would not criticize him if I found out about it.

•

It must be remembered that the American electoral campaign was then in full swing. My suspicions about Beheshti were soon confirmed. In this same period, an Iranian general named Bahman Bagheri came to see me. He offered to purchase documents proving that Beheshti had long-standing contacts with the CIA. The seller was none other than the daughter of Assadolah Alam, a former minister in the Shah's court. I answered that my office prevented me from acquiring such a report. This same General Bagheri, who is related to a U.S. senator, also told me that an Iraqi attack was being organized with U.S. support. Realizing that he could provide us with valuable information, I obtained permission from Khomeini for Bagheri to travel to the West. Even if he took advantage of the trip to flee the country or returned empty-handed, we would not be taking any great risk.

With orders in hand to purchase industrial products abroad, Bagheri went to the Tehran airport. He never left. Arrested by the Revolutionary Guards, he has been rotting in prison for years. I asked Khomeini what the reasons were for this arrest. "He lied," was the response. "So, where was the risk?" I asked. "Even if he had deceived us it would not have mattered."

This incident, plus several others, made me uneasy about Khomeini's possible involvement in the mullahs' plan.

What Beheshti wanted, of course, was to prevent Bagheri's departure for the United States, where he might discover damaging information. But what did Khomeini want if he was not in on it? It was simply to let this general leave because he might have been able to provide us with information.

On October 8, I received a visit from Sadegh Tabatabai, Ahmed Khomeini's brother-in-law. To my great surprise, he told me about a trip he had taken to West Germany on September 10 at Khomeini's order. He had met with certain Americans through the agency of Hans-Dietrich Genscher, then West Germany's foreign affairs minister. Tabatabai had been instructed to tell Warren Christopher, Carter's undersecretary of state for foreign affairs, that Khomeini, sick and afraid for his life, wanted to solve the hostage problem as quickly as possible. This was only a ruse, however, for while Tabatabai was in Germany, Khomeini was in excellent health. He had left the hospital, reassured about the state of his physical condition. It was, in fact, for this very reason that he had taken things in hand. Tabatabai was also instructed to advise Christopher that only three people in Iran knew about this trip. Since I was not one of the three, it was easy for me to guess who they were: Tabatabai himself plus Ahmed Khomeini and Hashemi Rafsanjani.

In fact, the message was clear: "Deal with me directly." Christopher and Carter did not understand. They thought, quite logically, that the three people referred to were Tabatabai, Khomeini, and Bani-Sadr, president of the Republic. Carter believed that we were a state run like any other. There was a president and it was to him that one should address oneself, as protocol demanded. This is what Carter did a short time later when he sent me new proposals, again through the West German ambassador to Tehran. But Carter was mistaken. He failed to realize that Khomeini did things his own way and had only one concern: power. As for me, I mistakenly believed, for a long time, that Khomeini and I enjoyed a father-and-son relationship.

I understood the meaning of Tabatabai's visit when I realized that he, in turn, had been cast aside. He had come to me for protection. He was afraid that this trip would be used to accuse him of being an "American agent."

After Tabatabai's confession and after Carter's proposals, it became increasingly obvious to me that Beheshti wanted to solve the hostage problem on someone else's behalf. That someone could only be Ronald Reagan.

On September 13, 1980, Khomeini made yet another about-face, forgetting that he had entrusted the resolution of the hostage affair to parliament. In a speech, he suddenly listed four conditions for the Americans' release. These were not the conditions we had relayed to Jimmy Carter. They were prepared by the Americans themselves. This was how Christopher had planned to obtain proof that Tabatabai was indeed the Imam's middleman.

At this time, Khomeini, as usual, was aiming at the two American presidential candidates, Ronald Reagan and Jimmy Carter, at the same time. He also wanted to make it clear that the real power in Iran resided exclusively in himself. Moreover, he was afraid of war and the American reaction. His objective, then, was to solve the hostage problem and prevent war. If successful, he would receive all the credit.

•

Time was growing short for everyone. Edmund Muskie, the U.S. secretary of state, told Reagan's people, "Get moving. Bani-Sadr is solving the problem." The general consensus at the time was that Carter's re-election depended entirely on resolution of the hostage problem at the American embassy.

KHOMEINI CHOOSES REAGAN

When the Iraqi attack finally came, Khomeini's position varied according to the situation on the front. In periods of crisis, he was more supportive of my proposals; at other times, when the danger of defeat seemed remote, he leaned toward the mullahs' arguments. He was a master at adapting to circumstances.

The yo-yo approach continued for a long time. About-faces followed one another at a dizzying rate. War consumes all energies. The hostages were no longer mentioned. Beheshti, in a press conference, clearly expressed the Imam's new attitude when he said that the hostage affair was of no great importance and that we had plenty of time to solve it. Parliament was busy handling more urgent matters, he concluded. It was obvious to me that Khomeini did not want me to reap the benefits of the hostages' release or a ceasefire on our terms.

He made the following calculations: in the United States, Reagan will replace Carter if the release of the hostages is delayed; in Iran, Bani-Sadr's position will be weakened and perhaps Saddam Hussein will be ousted by continuing the war. Thus, the mullahs would win on all fronts. If, after eliminating both the Shah and Carter, Khomeini causes the fall of Saddam Hussein—what an important role in history! For a clergyman from a Third World country to depose such important figures—what glory!

At the time, I had no idea that all these things were going through his mind. I thought that this was Beheshti's reasoning, not Khomeini's. When I was with him, I constantly mentioned the danger Reaganism would pose if the hostages were not released very quickly. I explained that Reagan's arrival would signify a change in the American mentality. From a post-Vietnam War mentality of everyone deciding his own fate, there would be a shift to the concept of intervention in the affairs of others. We should not contribute to Reagan's election.

Khomeini said, "So what if Reagan wins? Nothing will really change since he and Carter are both enemies of Islam." Actually, he knew the difference.

The day after Reagan's election, I wrote to Khomeini to remind him of his responsibility. "There is already talk of a 'Reagan solution' to the Iran problem. We are therefore responsible for everything that happens."

When, on October 15, we had completely contained the Iraqi army, I became truly dangerous to the mullahs. They therefore had to act. They knew that my Achilles' heel was the hostage problem. On that day, Rajai, the prime minister, went to the United Nations without consulting Khomeini or me. He apparently learned in New York that Iran was completely isolated because of the hostage affair, which we all knew. On his return trip, during a stopover in Algiers, Algerian diplomats made it clear to him that a solution was urgently needed.

Suddenly, Rajai announced on October 22 that Iran wanted neither American spare parts nor American arms. Rafsanjani repeated the same thing to Eric Rouleau, who published it in *Le Monde* on October 24, 1980. Strange, isn't it?

Everyone knew that we needed spare parts. The enemy was on our territory, we had used all our forces to contain it, and the head of parliament, a member of the Defense Council, was making a statement like this without consulting anyone! It became very clear to me that the Carter solution had been ruled out. Carter was offering the arms we had purchased during the Shah's reign; they were paid for and we desperately needed them. Actually, the mullahs were negotiating secretly with Reagan. To be sure, one of their conditions involved arms, but they could not at any cost be routed through me since they were intended for forces loyal to the mullahs, the Revolutionary Guards in particular.

Reagan's people and the mullahs agreed that the arms would be shipped as soon as Bani-Sadr was out of the picture. This is precisely what happened. The first contract was signed in early March 1981 and the first shipments arrived in July, immediately after my departure. The arrangements had been made around

•

October 22, the day Rajai made that mysterious statement about not wanting American arms. One had to read between the lines.

According to various inquiries and the statements of Richard Brenneke (see pp. 35–36), an arms merchant, the agreement between the mullahs and the Reagan team was concluded in Paris during the third week of October 1980. In a hearing before Judge Jim R. Carrigan in Denver, Colorado, on September 23, 1988, Brenneke corroborated the statements of Heinrich Rupp, a pilot and CIA agent accused of bank fraud who claimed to have flown several American officials—in particular, George Bush, the U.S. vice-presidential candidate, and William Casey, the future head of the CIA—to France a few weeks before the American elections. They allegedly met with Iranian envoys in Paris, first at the Hotel Crillon and then at the Hotel Raphaël, to negotiate the release of the hostages.

At his hearing, Brenneke affirmed having attended several meetings between William Casey and a representative of Rafsanjani. The Iranian he named was Cyrus Hashemi. The French, he claimed, particularly an agent named Robert Benes, were to handle the logistics. Of course, one of the conditions for the hostages' release was the provision of arms. A partial payment of $40 million would be made to the French, who would then be responsible for purchasing the equipment and delivering it to the Iranians.

Brenneke was not alone in speaking of this agreement between Reagan and the mullahs. Several reports mentioned meetings between the Iranian envoys and Reagan's emissaries. Before concluding the contract in Paris, the emissaries allegedly met in Washington. These reports mention three Iranians: Albert Hakim, who later played an important role in Irangate, Gorbanifar, and Cyrus Hashemi. Mention may also have been made of a representative of Beheshti's whose name I do not know. On several occasions the international press related this story, which I believe to be true, especially since in late October 1980 I received a report that some $30 million had been paid into Beheshti's account in Frankfurt.

The events that followed are known as "Irangate."

The hostage affair became the exclusive preserve of three individuals: Beheshti, Rafsanjani, and Ahmed Khomeini, with

•

Rajai as the executing agent and Behzad Nabavi the official negotiator with Carter.

UNITED STATES DISTRICT COURT
FOR THE DISTRICT OF COLORADO

....

UNITED STATES OF AMERICA   Docket No. 88-CR-112
  Plaintiff,   Denver, Colorado
                                  September 23, 1988

  v.

HEINREICH RUPP,
  Defendant.

....

PARTIAL REPORTER'S TRANSCRIPT
BEFORE THE HONORABLE JIM R. CARRIGAN

TRANSCRIPT ORDERED BY: The Rocky Mountain News

APPEARANCES:

For the Government:
Thomas O'Rourke, Assistant United States Attorney
Jeff Kinder, Assistant United States Attorney

For the Defendant:
Michael Scott, Esq.
Daniel Burerah, Esq.

Excerpts from the hearing on September 23, 1988, before Judge Carrigan of the United States District Court for the District of Colorado.

(Cover of the document)

Excerpt No. 1.

Brenneke: On October 19, Mr. Rupp brought Mr. Bush, Mr. Casey, and several other people to Paris, France, from the United States, to a meeting with Iranian representatives.

Question: Did you attend any of these meetings after the arrival of Mr. Casey, Mr. Bush, and the others?

Brenneke: Yes, Your Honor.

....

Brenneke: The meeting I attended was held at the Hotel Florida in Paris, France, on October 20, 1980. Some people I knew in France were present, an individual named Robert Benes.

Judge: How is that spelled?

Witness: B-E-N-E-S, Your Honor.

Judge: Is he French?

Witness: He is French. He is a Frenchman.

....

Brenneke: The purpose of these meetings was to negotiate not only the release of the hostages then being held at the United States Embassy in Tehran, but also to discuss, if the negotiations were successful, to discuss the means whereby the terms of the agreement would be . . . would be implemented, how we could satisfy everyone. Consequently, the French were there because they were to constitute an essential element in the satisfaction of the demands.

Finally, the agreement was concluded; the procedures were defined for a transfer of $40 million for the arms purchase. It was for this meeting that Mr. Rupp brought the vice president, then a candidate for the vice presidency, George Bush, and the future director of the CIA, Mr. Casey, to Paris.

Afterward, Casey went to Frankfurt and the vice president, who stayed less than 24 hours, returned to the United States. Several people remained in Paris to arrange for receipt of the funds placed at their disposal and to handle the logistics for delivery of the arms—the arms ultimately purchased with these funds—to the Iranians.

....

As a result of this meeting, certain Frenchmen purchased arms individually; in the end, they exchanged these arms for . . . or at least as one of the conditions for the release of the American hostages being held in Tehran.

....

Judge: So, you are saying that a payment of $40 million was made to the French—is that what you are saying?—and that the French purchased arms with it?

Witness: Yes. Approximately $40 million was placed in—excuse me—in different bank accounts in Europe, for the people who were going to buy and exchange the arms.

On October 24, Prosecutor General Mousavi Ardebili, former president (1989) of the Supreme Judicial Council and chief justice of the Court of Appeals, came to see me in Desfoul, on the front, after meeting with Khomeini. The tone was extremely conciliatory. I was therefore quite frank with him about the hostage problem, telling him that the agreement with the Americans, in its present form, was going to sink Carter. I told him that, according to Ghotbzadeh, Rajai, during his trip to the United States on October 22, had concluded the final agreement concerning the hostages, the terms of which had been worked out in Paris. His trip to the United Nations really had only one purpose: to make the agreement official. Ardebili replied that Ghotbzadeh had invented this story because of his own removal.

On October 29, I criticized Rajai's trip, which had been taken without my consent, and Ahmed Khomeini came running to me immediately. I discussed this agreement with him, but without alluding to his role in it, which I was aware of. I put my cards on the table: "If, between now and the American elections, the Imam retains Rajai as prime minister, it will mean that he has consented to my departure. Tell your father it is inconceivable to conclude an agreement with the Americans without demanding the spare parts and arms we have already paid for and which are collecting dust in American warehouses. If he wants to oust me, let him say so." Ahmed, the faithful messenger, went to repeat to his father everything that I had said.

The American elections were not far off and events were accelerating. As far as the war was concerned, I was in a strong position. We had checked the Iraqi advance despite our meager resources, and the Cuban foreign affairs minister had come as Saddam Hussein's messenger to offer us a ceasefire following a return to the border, which was precisely what we wanted. Politically, my prospects were not so bright. A hundred deputies had just signed a petition demanding my resignation. Beheshti had come to the front to size up his chances of taking charge of the army if I were removed as commander in chief. I knew at once that he had contacted some of the officers for this purpose.

The deputies' petition and Beheshti's trip to the front were connected to the hostage agreement. I sent two letters, one to

Khomeini and the other to Rafsanjani, recounting everything I knew about the conspiracy, without, of course, implicating the Imam. I condemned the tyranny of the mullahs, the agreement with the Americans, and Ghotbzadeh's arrest. In a television broadcast, Ghotbzadeh had very harshly criticized the regime and had especially denounced its collusion with Reagan. They chose this pretext to put before parliament a bill calling for the control of radio and television by three representatives, one from the judicial branch and the other two from the executive and legislative branches. Under this law, the president would have no control because the representative of the executive branch would be appointed by the government, with or without the president's approval.

In response to these excesses, I asked the people to fight back. They demonstrated in the streets for Ghotbzadeh's release. In addition, my wife called Khomeini's wife to tell her, "What a fine example of loyalty! Your husband imprisons a man who has worked with him for twenty years simply because he said what he thought." Three days later, Ghotbzadeh was released. However, this same Ghotbzadeh, who knew too much about the regime's intrigues with the Americans, contacted me in September 1981, while I was in exile in France, to tell me that he was planning to overthrow the regime. I gave him my opinion of this plot, which I thought was unrealistic and which I could not approve in principle. I later learned that he had asked the Iraqis to suspend action on the front while he seized control and that he had injudiciously contacted Saudi Arabia to request financial assistance. Relations between the Saudis and the Americans were such that the Reagan administration was immediately informed of the plan. Several days later, Ghotbzadeh was arrested and then executed on September 15, 1982.

Did the Americans denounce him to Khomeini? I don't know. I note only that he was arrested right after Michael Ledeen, a Reagan adviser, told a Frenchman who was visiting him, "One, we believe that the Iranian regime is stable. Two, it is not acting contrary to American interests. Three, we will not assist any coup d'état against it."

If Ghotbzadeh—who was my friend despite our long-standing political differences—had told me what he was doing,

I would have advised him not to contact the Saudis. Although certain military personnel and clerics such as Shariatmadari were among the organizers of the coup, it was the work of amateurs. Why alert the Americans? Especially if, as I believe, they had not asked the Americans for anything. I think it is fair to say that Ghotbzadeh was a victim of the hostage affair. He was intimately familiar with it because, as foreign affairs minister, he had met in Paris with Hamilton Jordan, a Carter adviser who had worn a disguise to the meeting.

In late October 1980, everyone was openly discussing the agreement with the Americans on the Reagan team. In the October 27 issue of *Enghelab Eslami*, I published an editorial saying that Carter was no longer in control of U.S. foreign policy and had yielded the real power to those who had pushed Saddam Hussein into the war and had negotiated with the mullahs in the hostage affair.

Caught as I was between the war and the hostages, my days were numbered. In this race against time, the war would have to end before the American elections on November 4, or at least before the new president's inauguration in late January 1981.

The days surrounding Reagan's election proved to be decisive in the history of this war, and every political trend existing in Iran today emerged during that period.

3

REAGAN SHORT-CIRCUITS CARTER

FROM NOVEMBER 4, 1980, THE DATE OF REAGAN'S ELECtion, to January 21, 1981, the date of his inauguration, a foursome was played between Carter and Reagan in the United States and between the mullahs and me in Iran.

On November 10, Khomeini's older brother Pasandideh wrote to parliament to express official support for the president of the Republic and to vehemently protest measures aimed at suppressing freedoms. The president of the Assembly did not dare to read this letter in open session, but it was published in *Enghelab Eslami*. The next day, the number of copies printed rose from 100,000 to 200,000, proving that the Iranian people were following the political conflicts on a daily basis.

On November 14, four moderate deputies admitted to me that, in effect, they had approved a solution of the hostage affair. They said that they were unfamiliar with the details of the agreement, but nevertheless thought that it was detrimental to Iran. I was frank with them. "It's more serious than you think. Now that Reagan has been elected, if the mullahs don't get rid of me, the agreement will be nullified. But if we manage to win this arm wrestling match, the White House will be forced to give us the arms they promised in exchange for the release of the hostages, which is going to happen very soon. If we get these weapons, we will win the war and eliminate the mullahs. Make no mistake, this is not just a simple disagreement between an intellectual and a cleric. By accepting the agreement with the Americans, these clerics have committed themselves to my elimination. They won't give up."

Khomeini had only one fear: that I would reveal the agreement to the people. He was afraid that I would do it on Ashura (the tenth day of the month of Moharram, when the third Imam was killed). I had organized a large rally in Tehran. When I arrived at Freedom Square in a helicopter, I saw a sea of humanity converging on the square. I had actually intended to tell everything and submit to the judgment of the people. Khomeini immediately assessed the risk he was running, even if I spared him in my speech. Before the ceremony, he warned me, "You must not mention these mullahs; leave them alone."

"That's the whole problem," I answered. "Why should I spare them when they constantly pressure you to demand my resignation and they draft petitions to discredit me with the people? They won't let up because they have signed an agreement with Reagan."

"Who told you about this agreement? What you are hearing is absurd," he answered.

I then asked, "Why can't you believe that such an agreement exists? In this case, just how far will you lower yourself? Your role in the revolution was vital, but the others—Beheshti, Rafsanjani— they came afterward and would be nothing without you. You know as well as I that most of these men were deeply involved in the Shah's regime and if they were thoroughly investigated, could wind up in prison." I then reminded him of Beheshti, who had obtained a position at the Hamburg mosque through the recommendation of the president of the senate and was paid a salary by the Pahlavi Foundation. There were even rumors that he had been appointed by *Savak* (the secret police), although I never had any proof. Nevertheless, the documents I saw show that the Pahlavi Foundation paid him money on a regular basis. Rafsanjani made a fortune during the Shah's reign by speculating in real estate, and the three of them—Behesthi, Rafsanjani, and Rajai—even formed a company.

"If these men are under the Americans' heel, it's their problem," I added. "They are nothing but traitors; but in your case, it's more serious. For the sake of the Iranian revolution and all Islam, how can you believe that I am going to accept your submission to the United States? That is precisely where Beheshti's road will take you."

In the end, I agreed to remain silent on the condition that Khomeini forbid the mullahs to continue their creeping coup d'état. I still wanted to trust him. "All right," he said, "I'll forbid it."

It all meant nothing, however, since Bazargan's newspaper was attacked the very next day. I also received a visit from the engineer, Ehzatollah Sahabi, a deputy and former member of the Revolutionary Council, who told me that Ardebili, the Court of Appeals prosecutor, had told him that the attack on *Mizan*, Bazargan's paper, was only a prelude to the banning of our newspaper *Enghelab Eslami*. My last means of expression was about to be taken away from me.

Khomeini had not kept his word. He simply wanted to buy my silence on Ashura. On November 20, Khomeini's grandson Hussein came to tell me what his grandfather was supposedly saying to everyone: "Bani-Sadr loses control of what he says and gets completely carried away. He often says things before thinking them through." The sole purpose of this, of course, was to upset me.

During this same period, the *Fedayeen-e-Khalq*, a Marxist organization, publicly accused me of Bonapartism. Consequently, they announced that they were joining forces with the mullahs, as the Tudeh Party had already done. This was a surprising alliance: pro-Soviets allied with pro-Americans! Their rationale was simple. In a democratic regime, there would be little room for them on the political chessboard. However, with the mullahs—who had no plan, no professionals, and embodied the past—it would be possible to infiltrate the social machinery. They were saying, quite clearly, "True, they made a deal with the United States, but that's good because it's their weak spot and we can exploit it."

•

It was therefore essential that I be eliminated. They chose to attack on all fronts, and I had to fight back. I could not allow myself to become what Khomeini eventually did—a phantom president, an impotent witness to all the crimes.

This agreement with the Reagan-Bush team plunged us into a state of internal warfare.

After I left Iran, I could not explain things very clearly because of the war. My duty was to respect the struggle for Iranian independence and not undermine the morale of those who were fighting for it. I especially hoped that Khomeini would one day reconsider his position. I waited eight years for him to do it. He never did. A leader can be forgiven many crimes, but never submission to a foreign power. A people can survive the crimes of their leaders, but not submission, which has caused so many civilizations to vanish. This agreement with Reagan led Iran into error because it promoted the establishment of Khomeiniism, an ideology based on the great principles of the revolution, but with the objectives changed.

We fought the revolution for independence, but what does this word connote? To make war, arms must be purchased, and for that, oil must be sold. Trade generally implies relations between countries able to exist as equals. But this agreement for the secret purchase of arms in exchange for lower oil prices led directly to economic, cultural, and political dependence. In the name of independence, Iran has become more dependent than it was under the Shah. The revolution was fought in the name of freedom, but freedom is only possible when the people's safety is assured both at home and abroad. The clerics have finally adapted the precepts of Islam to their predicament with the United States and, in the process, have created a system that permits every form of abuse.

The hostage affair was not only the Iranians' doing; it was also an incredible maneuver on the part of Reagan's supporters. The proof of this, in my opinion, is that whenever a solution of the problem was near, the Americans always created obstacles. Carter recently admitted that he was aware of the contacts between Reagan's aides and those of Khomeini. As for me, I thought that certain elements in the Carter administration had allied themselves with the Reagan camp and were leaking information to it. I later learned that to prevent an "October surprise" (the release of the hostages in October, a month before the American elections), Reagan had organized two working committees with no holds barred.

The mullahs were at this time split into two factions, one on the Left and the other on the Right. The Left was primarily Stalinist and leaned toward the Soviet Union, while the Right was also Stalinist but leaned toward the United States. Both of these groups agreed on one point: to use leftist organizations to drive me from office. Beyond that, however, there was no consensus. The attack on June 28, 1981, that caused the death of Beheshti and numerous officials of the Islamic Republic Party was undoubtedly the result of one group fighting the other. A similar attack could have been made against me. They also planned to kill me at that time. The army intercepted conversations about my assassination on the Kermanshah front. One mullah even issued a *fatwa* (religious sanction) to kill me.

A RACE AGAINST TIME

On the Reagan team, a certain impatience held sway. One of my advisers, who is now in the United States, was contacted several times by the president's aides. They wanted me to endorse the agreement. The problem stemmed from the fact that Reagan had just been elected and I was still in office. They needed an official spokesman to honor the quid pro quo of the agreement, that is, the arms shipment. Rashid Sadrol Hefazi, the director of information services in the president's office, acted as intermediary. He was executed after the coup against me because he knew too much about the ties between Beheshti, Rafsanjani, Reagan, and Bush. He received telephone calls at my office from Americans saying, "I am calling on behalf of Mr. Reagan. We would like to discuss the hostage problem." I instructed him to answer: "The president is dealing with this problem at the intergovernmental level and, to the best of our knowledge, Mr. Carter is the head of the United States government until January 20. We will only negotiate through official channels and not over the telephone with people who say they represent Reagan."

•

Sadrol Hefazi, the man who knew too much, was executed without a trial after making a confession on television.

Why, in this period, was Reagan so intent on contacting me despite my persistent refusals? He knew that this secret agreement would have to be ratified one way or another by the time he entered the White House. If I were to state officially that I knew nothing about the agreement, how could it be carried out? What a scandal that would be! It was therefore essential that I either be eliminated or included in the arrangement. This is why he was in such a hurry.

I could have taken this opportunity to turn the secret agreement to my advantage. But it would have been contrary to the values of the revolution, especially the principle of independence. Then, too, Khomeini would have been able to eliminate me afterward by accusing me of being a collaborator. Finally, it was impossible because I believed that the future of the Iranian revolution and our restored independence demanded that none of the leaders of the revolution capitulate to foreign powers. For these three reasons, I declined the offer of the new American president.

To camouflage and strengthen the agreement with Reagan, the mullahs were forced to enter into official negotiations with Carter, who was still in office. These negotiations continued from November 20, 1980, until January 20, 1981, the day before Reagan's inauguration. In October, Beheshti was still saying, "We are in no hurry to solve the hostage problem; there is plenty of time." And then, all of a sudden, just after November 4 (Reagan's election), it became urgent for him to negotiate.

During these official negotiations with Carter, no report was made to me—not a word. Behzad Nabavi, the government-appointed negotiator, later tried in an interview to discredit me with the people, who were shocked by this agreement, which they considered unfavorable to Iran. He wanted to make me responsible by saying that I had followed the discussions from day to day and that I had done nothing to stop them. My office emphatically denied this, and Nabavi, unable to come up with anything better, said that he had not had the time to inform the president of the terms of the agreement with Carter. Everyone knew, however, that according to Article 125 of the Constitution, my signature was required on all international agreements.

•

On November 12, 1980, an Algerian delegation arrived in Iran with American proposals for resolving the hostage affair. Fourteen days later, on November 26, Iran responded. As in a football game, the Iranian negotiators were playing against the clock. Obviously, they wanted to drag things out with Carter. Warren Christopher, Carter's representative, wanted to expedite the negotiations. Messages flew back and forth between Tehran and the United States via the Algerian diplomats.

On December 11, Iran was still insisting on two conditions for the release of the hostages: that it be clearly understood, first of all, that no one—not the hostages, their families, or the American government—would seek damages; and second, that an estimate of the assets of the Shah and his family be made. According to Nabavi, Iranian advisers had estimated the Shah's assets in the United States at more than $56 billion.

On December 12, the Americans responded. Pressed for time, they agreed to the first demand but considered estimating the Shah's assets in the United States to be impossible without an inquiry. Any such inquiry would, of course, take more time than Carter had remaining in office.

On December 17, Behzad Nabavi asked the Americans—again, through the Algerians—to deposit $24 billion in a bank account as security for the Shah's assets and the frozen Iranian funds. There was only one reason for this shameful blackmail: to stall for time. Neither Carter nor I were dupes. The Carter administration, not wanting to burn its bridges, accepted the offer. On December 21, contact was renewed with the Algerians, who returned to the United States.

On January 15, Nabavi suddenly threw the engines into reverse. Not only did he renounce the $24 billion, he agreed to pay all of Iran's external debts in cash. The mere fact of paying in cash gave the Americans $500 million. What a windfall! How could such a reversal have come about?

With only six days remaining until Reagan's inauguration, everyone aware of the secret agreement with the future president clearly understood this maneuver. Nabavi was making last-minute sacrifices to guarantee the success of the agreement and the release of the hostages as a gift to Ronald Reagan on the day of his inauguration.

•

Events therefore accelerated, and on January 17, in Algiers, Nabavi signed the final agreement. The Iranian people realized that the only result of these two and a half months of negotiations was that the hostages were freed without any reciprocal action on the part of the United States. It did not take all that time just to achieve this outcome. The Americans could have been handed this gift on the very first day, except that the hostages would have gone home while Carter was in office. On January 19, after the agreement was signed, Nabavi sent the decree to me for approval. This was only a formality since the agreement had already been signed. Since I had said that I would reject any agreement not favorable to Iran, they had attempted to circumvent my veto by calling their agreement the "Algiers Declaration." I remained an obstacle, however, because to honor the second part of the agreement with Reagan, payment was necessary. For that, several signatures, including my own, were essential.

The closer January 21 came, the more I was attacked. But the president of the central bank, my friend Nobari, was an even bigger target than I. Prime Minister Alireza Rajai wrote to me, demanding Nobari's resignation. The newspapers denounced him every day. He had been called before the revolutionary tribunals on several occasions, but since they could not get rid of him without my approval, they went to the trouble of passing a law in parliament to replace him. On January 17, the day the Algier's Declaration was signed, I wrote to Khomeini, "This declaration is a shameful declaration, a capitulation, and it will be remembered as such in history. You must act quickly to prevent its signature."

On January 21, as Reagan was taking the oath of office, the aircraft carrying the hostages took off from Tehran. The first phase of the agreement was honored. If a comparison of all these dates were made, it would be seen that they coincide exactly with the steps Rafsanjani's group took to get rid of me.

On January 22, 1981, Beheshti and Rafsanjani both said essentially the same thing. Beheshti declared, "We have found our way, our people have found their way, the State has found its way, and this unified whole is working in coordination. The hostage problem had to be resolved eventually."

In other words, the hostages were needed to create this

•

unified whole, and now that they were no longer needed, they were being released. Rafsanjani said the same thing, but was more specific. "Parliament, the government, and the judiciary are all working together with the Imam, and we are unanimous in saying that if the hostages had not been taken, the United States would have found some other way of forcing the Iraqis to attack."

These two statements make one thing clear: the purpose of taking the hostages was to unify the power structure.

REAGAN SEEKS AN OFFICIAL SPOKESMAN

Soon after the inauguration, the Reagan administration put the ayatollahs on notice that they had better hurry up and get the country's internal problems solved. The rest of the agreement could not be carried out without an official spokesman. In one of his first speeches, in early February, Reagan said, "In Iran, there is no government to deal with." The message was clear. They did not want the agreement to take effect if any part of the power structure in Iran could reject it.

Reagan's statement was dangerous for me because Khomeini, feeling himself threatened, might decide to attack. I immediately asked my advisers to prepare a document denouncing the government's position. We drafted a detailed indictment of the Algiers Declaration, its signers, Behzad Nabavi, and Prime Minister Rajai, and then we submitted it to the courts.

On February 5, our country's financial experts revealed that the agreement was costing us several billion dollars. The newspapers printed this information, and Nabavi was extremely embarrassed. He tried to minimize everything by telling the press: "Put away your calculators. The purpose of the hostage affair was not to make or lose money; there were other stakes. The financial losses don't count."

A recent opinion poll showed that 90 percent of the Iranian people believe that the conclusion of the hostage affair was detrimental to Iran.

On January 29, 1981, the Algerian ambassador came to see me to discuss the Reagan administration's new policy. I criticized the position of his government, which had endorsed this traitorous

•

agreement. "On the contrary," he replied, "We explained to Nabavi that this agreement was not good for Iran, but he told us he would sign it anyway. We were intermediaries in the agreement with Carter, but not the other one, the one Beheshti and Rafsanjani concluded with Reagan." He also insisted that I would have to end the war very quickly if I wanted to remain in office.

This warning coincided with the forty-page document I had received on January 10, 1981. It was a plan to eliminate me, involving a change of regime. Part of the text was written for grass-roots organizers. It was fairly innocuous since they had assumed it might fall into my hands anyway. The other, more confidential part contained explicit plans for my physical elimination. Reference was made to an automobile accident in Khuzestan. It even called for the announcement of a forty-day official mourning period the day following my death. For the second time, the document indicated that a *fatwa* had been issued against me.

Apparently, Reagan was in a big hurry. He wanted to avoid a scandal at the beginning of his term. Irangate, his arms sales to the mullahs, revealed to the world by a leak within the regime, would later prove that his anxiety was justified. The Islamic Republic Party understood the message in Reagan's speech. Bani-Sadr's elimination had to be accelerated.

On March 15, 1981, Khomeini invited Bazargan, Beheshti, Rafsanjani, Mousavi Ardebili, Khameini, Rajai, his son Ahmed, and me to his home. At the end of the meeting, the Imam asked each of us to write down on a piece of paper one thing that we had set our hearts on. Afterward, I said, "I know what Rafsanjani and Beheshti wrote; do you want me to tell you?" They answered yes, of course.

"They wrote: it's not working; it's Bani-Sadr or us; and we say us, so Bani-Sadr has to go."

Everyone smiled while Ahmed unfolded the papers. Then he laughed out loud because that was exactly what Beheshti and Rafsanjani had written. I then drew the conclusion for everyone, "Reagan has spoken."

The purpose of Khomeini's invitation was to ease tensions, to get me and the others to sign a truce, as he put it. He was afraid

•

that if the whole thing were aired in public, the mullahs would be discredited.

In early February, the judge with whom I had filed my complaint against the authors of the Algiers Declaration came to see me. According to him, the case was so strong that he was going to issue warrants for the arrest of Prime Minister Rajai and Nabavi. I told him, "Fine, go ahead." I of course doubted that this would actually happen and was proved right. The next day, the file was seized by Mousavi Ardebili, who turned it over it to an arbitration committee appointed by Khomeini (at Bazargan's suggestion) to settle the differences between the mullahs and me. There was no justification for this change in procedure since the committee had only a political function and the complaint had been filed with the courts. Behzad Nabavi went to see Rajai to persuade him that this challenge to the Algiers Declaration was a Bani-Sadr coup d'état. They asked parliament to meet in closed session and for four hours demonstrated to the deputies that this complaint was actually aimed at Beheshti, Rafsanjani, and the Imam himself. Nabavi, who feared for his life, then made the following remark, heavy with meaning: "Bani-Sadr filed this complaint in order to reveal everything in court. He knows very well that we only follow orders. Why attack us?"

Although posing as the leaders' defender, Nabavi was indirectly threatening them. He implied that if the suit were successful, they would have to tell all—a clever move designed to protect himself. I asked the president of parliament to send me the tape recording of this session, which he of course refused. This tape proved that Nabavi knew about the agreement.

On March 15, one of my advisers, Hossein Navab Safavi, wrote an editorial criticizing Beheshti, who wanted to retaliate by dragging me into court.

"If anyone should be brought to justice, it's you. There are reports concerning your contacts with American agents dating from before the revolution. We know about your meetings with the American general, Huyser, with General Gharabaghi, the Shah's chief of staff, and with Sullivan, the American ambassador. Many other less important contacts with representatives of the 'Great Satan' are being prosecuted, why not yours? A year before the revolution you spent a great deal of time in the United States, traveling around and making political contacts. You therefore lack the necessary qualifications to be chief justice of the Court of Appeals."

When this editorial was published, the embassy documents were as yet unknown. Some of the ones concerning Beheshti still have not been made public. I saw some, but not all. According to my sources, there are many more concerning Mousavi Ardebili and the others. Navab Safavi, the author of this article, paid for his audacity with his life. He was arrested and executed after I left Iran. Unfortunately, he was not to be the only casualty among those who knew about the agreement and the contacts with the Americans. Certain individuals, such as Said Sanjabi and Ali Reza Nobari, the director of the central bank, managed to escape.

Despite my emphatic denunciation of the agreements with the Americans, on April 10, 1981, another of my advisers was contacted in West Germany by Reagan's representatives. It was the day after the signing of the first arms purchase contract with the Israelis. As president of the Republic and commander in chief of the armed forces, I was not officially aware of this contract. I had only been unofficially informed about it by the military. The quid pro quo of the agreement, that is, the delivery of arms, was being carried out, and I was still in office. It was becoming increasingly risky for the Americans to play this game, especially since funds transfers could not be made without my being informed of it for the director of the central bank was still Ali Reza Nobari, one of my most well-known friends. My answer to Reagan was again unequivocal. I refused any unofficial rapprochement. This attempt to establish secret relations with me was to be the last.

On April 12, I wrote to Mousavi Ardebili, the Court of Appeals prosecutor. I had all the evidence, documents, contracts, and testimony necessary to prove the contacts established with the "Great Satan." "For a year, I have been collecting information and I am now able to reveal what has been perpetrated against this republic. The Americans have repeatedly contacted several individuals in the Iranian government. Most recently, they contacted an individual—whom I shall not name—to discuss the establishment of a stable regime in Iran founded on a coalition

•

between the military and the clerics. They have also tried to establish secret relations with me. What they want, actually, is to prove to their people and to the world at large that we are racing to conclude an agreement with them, each group trying to outdistance the other. They want to show that the key to power is always in their hands."

This document was important because, for the first time, it officially exposed the agreement between Reagan, Rafsanjani, Bush, and Beheshti. No one asked me for any explanations concerning this letter. I was making serious, fully substantiated accusations; consequently, they did not react.

With an uproar like this on his hands, Khomeini was worried. The conciliation meeting at his home was proof. The circumstances were not favorable for my immediate removal, and the truce was a way of gaining time. I am still undecided about his role in the mullahs' plans because his behavior was inconsistent. He attacked me through third parties and, at the same time, confirmed me as the supreme commander of the war and abolished the Defense Council, which had been created specifically to block me. His son Ahmed claimed to be entirely on my side. What, then, was I to think? The mullahs kept increasing the pressure on Khomeini by playing up the fact that my popularity was greater than his. They urged him to act, almost by threatening him. They told him the following, which was reported to me by members of his entourage: "If you fought the revolution to make the clergy more subordinate than it was under the Shah, that is your business. The time to get rid of Bani-Sadr is now or never because he is winning the war. Afterward, you will not be able to oppose him."

They were pressed for time because of the agreement and the contracts with the Israelis for the purchase of American arms. The whole thing could blow up in broad daylight if the war ended.

Khomeini was caught in a bind. On the one hand, I had the support of the people, who might cry scandal, but on the other hand, the mullahs would not hesitate to implicate him if I triumphed.

Khomeini chose the lesser of two evils and deprived me of my office on June 10, 1981. By the purest of chances, the arms contracts signed in March 1981 were carried out in July, a few weeks after I went underground. Irangate was waiting to explode.

To the very end, the hostage affair—and its counterpart, the arms contracts—would poison the regime. Its repercussions are still a key element in the internal politics of Iran today.

4

FACE-OFF WITH THE MULLAHS

IN SEPTEMBER 1980, WE ALL KNEW THAT THE IRAQI ATTACK was imminent, and yet the political disputes, the ideological battles, and the low blows exchanged by the factions in power continued as never before. It was then that the mullahs became interested in the economy. They attacked the banks so viciously in the Friday prayers that every account was subsequently emptied. At the same time, Saudi Arabia, which had previously not dared to oppose the oil price increases we had won, suddenly decided to increase production. The purpose of this maneuver was to make us lose our markets because of our excessively high prices and to force us to lower production. We were caught between the economic blockade and the drop in oil export prices. Simultaneously, Beheshti decided to become an ultra-socialist. At the outset of the revolution he had organized the liberal Bazaar system, but his current interests dictated that he become the most thoroughly socialist of all Iranians. It was essential that he win the support of the revolutionary organizations.

In every sector of social life, the mullahs promoted the revolutionary organizations and the *maktabis*. The totalitarian mullahs divide society into four separate categories: the maktabis, those who are completely obedient to the faqih and can rightly be called the fanatics of the system; the semi-fanatics; the neutrals; and the opposition.

The maktabis must govern; the "semi-fanatics" can have responsibilities, but not key positions. The other two categories are not entitled to any degree of power. How can you govern with maktabis when you know that their philosophy is based on the pursuit of martyrdom? Man's life on earth does not count; only the afterlife matters. How you die is critical. If you die as Khomeini prescribes, you go to heaven, even if you have committed many sins. If you die in some other fashion, heaven will be closed to you forever, even if your life is exemplary.

It is no coincidence that Khomeini justified his acceptance of UN Security Council Resolution 598 by saying, "They speak of our dead, our missing. They fail to realize that, having died for Islam, they are in heaven." This fundamental idea implies absolute faith in the Imam, since it is he who indicates how to die. The supremacy of faith over development is therefore natural.

During this period, the newspapers published numerous articles pointing out the discrepancies between Khomeini and me. Bani-Sadr asks the question: How can we increase production? And Khomeini asks another: How can we strengthen our faith? From this philosophy of death stems the priority of war over peace, of the believer over the technician, of obedience over the acceptance of responsibilities.

However, while the immediate goal of the Iranian revolution was to overthrow a regime based on cultural isolation, repression, and foreign economic control, its true objectives were the fulfillment of human potential and the development of society. It is easy to see why Khomeini did not follow me. The question "How should one live?" is foreign to his system of beliefs and is compatible neither with absolute obedience nor with the religious regime he wanted to impose.

Seizing upon these contradictions, the mullahs had a field day with propaganda. They launched what was called the war of priorities, targeting specialists in particular. Assigning priority to science and technical specialization meant one thing: an army of professionals. Giving priority to faith, however, implied the formation of an army with the Revolutionary Guards. Rafsanjani became the champion of the war of priorities. He insisted every day that I sounded just like the Pahlavis. "Bani-Sadr does not dare use the word modernism, so he talks about science and technology, but he really means the same thing as the Pahlavis." This was completely untrue. No Muslim can forget that man is born to realize his potential; the man who does not develop himself is not a believer. These arguments had less impact than the points Beheshti was scoring with impatient youths. "Bani-Sadr wants to industrialize Iran, but the West has a lead of several centuries. How can we be expected to catch up? Instead, we, God's army, will impose our will on the West; we will force it to make its technology available to us." War is therefore a blessing and must be propagated everywhere.

Science versus faith. Actually, the conflict boiled down to two propositions: how to die versus how to live.

Khomeini and I also differed on foreign policy. I wanted Iran to regain the favorable opinion it had enjoyed during the revolution by reinstating freedom and abandoning all of the violent methods that had made us an outcast among nations. For the mullahs, unfortunately, public opinion did not exist. Khomeini explained his point of view to me quite clearly. "You are always talking about the 11 million people who voted for you, but there is no such thing as public opinion, neither in Iran nor anywhere else. It is a fabrication. Look at how the West created a Zionist state in the Middle East. They drove the Palestinians from their homeland, and no one said anything because they had created public opinion favorable to Israel in their various countries. Daring to criticize Israel to the West is impossible. It is plain to see that governments manufacture public opinion out of nothing and manipulate it at will." This theory basically implies that the people understand nothing. It is taken directly from the philosophy of Aristotle, who said that some men are born to govern, others to be governed. A few are aware and the rest are sheep; Plato said the same thing.

I asked Khomeini repeatedly, "If, as you say, the people understand nothing, how is it that they rose up against the Shah? Remember, it was not you who incited them to revolt. Your first statement was broadcast after the popular uprising." The people: conscious or unconscious? This was yet another source of contention between the two sides in our revolution. The mullahs concluded that my election was a mistake since the people, by definition, know nothing.

For all of these reasons, I was constantly talking, constantly explaining myself. I wanted the people to understand the danger of dictatorship, and if there are increasingly powerful antitotalitarian currents in Iran today, it is partly because of these explanations.

ARRESTS, EXECUTIONS, TORTURE

A few weeks before the war, the relations between the men in the regime had deteriorated. Forces militating in favor of dictatorship were gaining strength. There was no longer any possibility of exchanging ideas; we were in a state of extremely harsh confrontation. The regime had become an organism split in two by a spreading cancer. We had moved beyond the stage of simple political antagonism between the Islamic Republic Party and me. When the confrontation with this party subsided, another faction— remote-controlled by the mullahs—stepped in to oppose me, and so on.

I began to realize that the linchpin of this entire mechanism was Khomeini himself, who was manipulating small groups and encouraging them to resist in order that he might have an enemy and thereby justify dictatorship. For me, this internal opposition was the greatest danger. The mullahs had intensified their undermining of the administration by eliminating more and more technical professionals. For them, anyone who had studied abroad could not become a minister, unless he was a maktabi. Anyone who talked of specialization was a secret partisan of the American line. They unleashed such waves of propaganda that many professionals left Iran at once. These clerics were not really opposed to modernism, as was believed here in the West; they were simply in a rush to seize total control.

I developed a strategy to dispel the mystery surrounding the clerics, the revolutionary organizations, the judicial apparatus, and the propaganda machine. It was essential that these myths be destroyed, that the truth about the machinations of these mullahs be told. I did it first in *Enghelab Eslami*—the circulation of which doubled, tripled, and then quadrupled—and then, because I had no access to radio and television, which I distrusted anyway, I invented Radio-Bazaar.

I made the people active participants in politics. In meetings, rallies, and editorials, I constantly repeated, "What I say, what I write, you, the people, must verify. I call on you to accept responsibility for verification. You know why Adam was banished from paradise; it was not because he disobeyed. God is not a tyrant. It was because he failed to ask questions when Satan tempted him to eat the fruit that was supposed to make him God's equal. He yielded without thinking, whereas he should have been wary and should have asked why the devil had not eaten the fruit himself. He didn't even ask God why He had forbidden him to eat the fruit.

"You, the people, if you do not ask questions, you will be like your father Adam: banished from the paradise of the revolution. What is in store for you is the worst of dictatorships. The Pahlavi dictatorship started the flight of expertise; this one will bring about its extermination. It is your duty to spread the truth."

That was Radio-Bazaar. A people who fail to use their critical sense cannot progress. This system operated for a long time.

In my columns, in my speeches, I developed the idea that Islam must be viewed as a method of promoting the progress of man in today's society, of making him a dynamic individual, accepting of both risk and re-evaluation. I created a slogan for this: "The people in the political arena: free, active, critical, involved, responsible." This slogan sparked a new ideological battle between the partisans of traditional Islam and the supporters of a dynamic Islam. It continues today: Khomeini was fond of saying that the people must be present in the political arena, but it must be added that for him their presence signified approval.

I chose as the focus of this campaign the principles I believed in—freedom, independence, and so on—as well as another topic that had become red-hot: the prisons. Under the Shah, there were two kinds of prisons: Savak prisons and ordinary prisons. In late 1980, there were several other kinds as well. I counted five different types of prisons in addition to the ordinary civil law prisons: the prisons of the Revolutionary Guards, those of the revolutionary tribunals, those of the political parties, those of the Guardians of the Observance of Islamic Principles, and those of the town committees.

In all of these prisons, torture was commonplace. One day in this period I was visited by a representative of Amnesty International. I confirmed his fears without hesitation. I even urged him to loudly denounce the torture and brutality in our prisons. I was willing to speak frankly with him because I had worked with his organization during the Shah's reign. I needed a denunciation like this to put an end to the excesses. Khomeini later reproached me for having publicly stated that torture existed in Iran and for having discredited Islam and the clerics. "No," I answered, "it is you who discredit the revolution by condoning violence." Denouncing these excesses proves that it is not the aim of the revolution to replace one set of torturers with another.

It was in these circumstances that war would break out, bringing into direct confrontation two peoples, two regimes, and, more particularly, two men: Saddam Hussein and Khomeini.

5

OLD ACQUAINTANCES

Saddam Hussein and Khomeini

THE CONTACTS BETWEEN KHOMEINI AND SADDAM HUSSEIN are long-standing; the relations between the two men played an important role in the war.

On November 4, 1964, Khomeini was deported to Turkey by the Shah. Khomeini then settled in Iraq, in the city of Najaf, a famous Shiite academic center. Closely watched by the Iraqi regime and Savak, Khomeini's isolation was increased by the fact that the city's Shiite community was hostile to him. He attributed much more importance to himself as a religious leader than he actually possessed. He had, for example, suggested to Ayatollah Hakim, a high dignitary of the Iraqi Shiite hierarchy, that he—Hakim—take over the battle for Islam since Khomeini felt that he had fought long enough himself. Hakim reacted very negatively to this proposal and replied, "You may have fought, but not well." Khomeini was alone in Najaf, a city itself cut off from the Shiite world by the Baathist regime. In this situation, he could neither befriend the Iraqis nor abandon his utter opposition to the Shah without being forgotten.

It was in this period, in 1966, that Iranians living abroad—exiles like me—played a vital role in protecting Khomeini from

Iraqi threats. We had established him as a respected religious leader in Iran. His banishment to Najaf ultimately led to the Shah's downfall, for Khomeini would never have been able to mobilize the people had he remained in Iran. An initial coup attempt in 1963 had failed. The support of exiled Iranians served as a tremendous springboard to Khomeini. The Iraqis realized that Khomeini was not alone and that Iran acknowledged him.

Universal opposition to the Shah—Marxists included—strengthened Khomeini both strategically and tactically. Saddam Hussein therefore tried to contact him through an Iranian prince living in Paris, Mossafar Firous. He knew that by approaching him from Europe, Khomeini would be more favorably disposed toward an emissary to Najaf. Firous, however, did not involve himself directly. He called on a woman in his family, a former member of the Tudeh Party, who became a messenger to the Imam for both himself and the Iraqis. Before leaving Paris, the woman asked Ghotbzadeh for a letter of introduction to Khomeini. Ghotbzadeh complied, but wrote in the sealed letter that under no circumstances was the Imam to trust the bearer of the message.

In Najaf, she went to see Khomeini, who read her letter impassively and allowed her to repeat Saddam Hussein's message. The Iraqi regime proposed recognizing Khomeini as the spiritual leader of all Shiites, lifting all restrictions so that Najaf might again become the great university it had once been, and making available to him all the propaganda media—radio, television, newspapers—he wanted. It went even further and offered to finance a military organization loyal to the Imam. Saddam Hussein requested only one thing in exchange: that Khomeini collaborate with the Iraqi regime. Obviously, he wanted to use Khomeini to destabilize the Shah's regime. Khomeini, of course, did not respond. Saddam repeated his proposals several times, in particular through General Bakhtiar, Shahpour's cousin, who was also in exile in Iraq. Khomeini never allowed himself to be tempted.

After all these failures, the Iraqis took a hard line and expelled Iranians who had lived in their country for generations. In Iran, the newspapers accused Khomeini of not protesting the expulsions. In fact, he had sent two very strongly worded telegrams to the Iraqi government; to no avail, of course.

•

Despite this hostile environment, I went to Najaf in 1972 to see Khomeini. His eldest son, who has since died, told me that the Iraqis were willing to offer me four hours of radio time every day because they considered me one of the few who could make effective broadcasts against the Shah. I took advantage of my stay in Iraq to observe the country, and I noted that the Shah's regime was no different from what I saw there. I concluded that coming to Iraq to make propaganda against the Shah would be ridiculous.

One of Saddam Hussein's aides came to see us during the early days of the popular uprising. I told him that Khomeini and I refused to join forces with one dictatorship in order to fight another. Neither of us thought much of the Iraqi regime, with the difference that his son and many of his followers were working indirectly with the Iraqis. A certain Doâï received 50 dinars a month from the Iraqi secret police for his radio broadcasts entitled "The Voice of the Clerics." Doâï, Iran's ambassador to Baghdad at the beginning of the revolution, is now editor of the newspaper *Ettelaat* in Tehran.

KHOMEINI UNDER SURVEILLANCE

In 1975, a new course was taken and relations between the Shah and Saddam Hussein improved as a result of their recent signing of the famous Algiers Agreements, which were supposed to end the two countries' century-old border dispute over the Shatt-al-Arab waterway.

The Iranian opposition, tolerated until then, was rejected. The collaborators were discredited and Khomeini's intransigence was rewarded by increased popularity in Iran. He was spoken of everywhere as a religious leader who had not compromised with the Baathist regime.

Saddam Hussein, who did not dare expel Khomeini from Najaf, strongly advised him to keep quiet. And it must be admitted that he was circumspect, except on the occasion of the celebrations in Persepolis in 1973, when he organized a massive campaign to boycott the festivities. Georges Pompidou, president of the French Republic, had accepted the Shah's invitation. One of my friends, Ahmad Salamatian, therefore contacted Claude Mauriac

•

and a lawyer named Ducrot, both of whom were friends of the French president, and asked them to persuade Pompidou not to go to Persepolis. To back up our request, we sent a complete file to the president's office, detailing the crimes of the Iranian regime. After reading it, Georges Pompidou decided to cancel his trip and to send Jacques Chaban-Delmas in his place. The Shah was furious. Khomeini declared attendance at the celebrations illegal on religious grounds. The Iranian people did not appreciate the ostentatious display of wealth and many observers, both within the country and without, viewed these festivities as a sign of the regime's weakness.

Until the first disturbances in Iran, Khomeini was not very active. The initiative for the uprising came from the people themselves. Khomeini's involvement did not come until much later, despite our many efforts to break through his resistance. I wrote several reports but they had no effect on him because he had not analyzed the situation correctly and was afraid that the people would not follow him.

To aid the Shah's dying regime, the Iraqis were only too glad to intervene, which they did on the occasion of the first interview Khomeini ever granted to Western reporters. He had always refused to meet with the international press, claiming that he spoke no foreign languages and had no competent translator in Najaf. He said he was afraid that his words would be twisted. Those of us in Paris, however, knew the truth: He had nothing to say. We therefore collected the reporters' questions in Paris and prepared the answers, which we then sent to Najaf.

On leaving the interview, two Frenchmen, Maurice Séveno and Jean-Pierre Locatelli, were arrested by Saddam Hussein's police, who confiscated their tapes; but since they had copies that the Iraqis did not find, the newspaper *Le Monde* published the interview soon after Khomeini's arrival in Paris.

KHOMEINI EXPELLED

Shortly after this incident, Khomeini was expelled from Iraq. We thought at the time that his expulsion was simply the fulfillment of a secret clause in the Algiers Agreements. We now know that it was nothing of the kind, because two of the documents seized at the American embassy prove that this expulsion had a specific objective. According to the authors of these two memorandums, Khomeini was to be sent to Europe, where he would reveal just how backward his thinking was. This would be followed by a crisis in Iranian public opinion; the intellectuals would desert him and his popularity would plummet. It was for this reason alone that Saddam Hussein, cooperating with the Shah, expelled Khomeini.

Turned back at the Kuwaiti border, Khomeini was forced to find another place to live. He stayed in Algeria for a time, but he preferred Paris, although I thought that he would choose Hamburg, the site of the only Shiite mosque in Europe. He came to live near me in Cachan, in the Paris suburbs, despite the fact that in religious fundamentalist circles, Paris is regarded as a debauched city. By announcing that he was going to live near me, he wanted to give his seal of approval to the Islamic intellectual circle I represented. On the day of his arrival in Paris, his brother gave an interview in Tehran to reassure the public by saying that the Imam was going to live with Bani-Sadr, a renowned Islamicist.

I did not learn of these documents describing the trap set for Khomeini until much later, but I knew that Paris is one of the centers of world public opinion and that the penalty for making inane statements in this city is a rapid descent into oblivion. Many exiles with nothing to say have learned this bitter lesson. We therefore prepared a nineteen-point political platform and I carefully explained to Khomeini that he had to adhere to it if he wanted to preserve his credibility. Elaborating on it or digressing from it could cost him his reputation and his future. He understood this, and his political life began. He was, however, the most ungrateful man in the world. He owed everything to the revolutionary program and those who developed it. Imagine him left to his fate in Paris; in no time, he would have been saying anything that came into his head. The revolution might have continued, but without him.

This is how the revolutionary program was developed.

Every day in Neauphle-le-Château, I wrote an analysis of the situation for him. Khomeini became the Guide of the Revolution, the Shah left, and we went home.

•

Saddam Hussein sent us a new emissary. This time it was the grandson of a very highly respected Iranian religious leader. I have never before recounted this episode involving Saddam, Khomeini, and me. Saddam Hussein quite simply offered to apologize publicly for what happened in Najaf and for the Imam's expulsion, on the condition that Khomeini accept this friendly gesture. I went to Qom to present Saddam Hussein's request and was received privately by Khomeini. He remained inflexible.

"That dictator will last no more than six months because he is threatened by a revolution like ours. He wants to find a way out by making us this offer. I will not justify that pig." I replied that nothing prevented our accepting his apologies and that doing so did not mean that we were justifying him. He closed the interview by saying, "I'll think about it." In fact, this attempt at reconciliation hardened his resolve. Disinclined to forget a grievance and viewing Saddam Hussein's offer as a sign of weakness, Khomeini chose to hit his regime harder than ever. The message had the opposite effect from the one intended.

During the hostage affair, while I was foreign affairs minister, the Iraqi ambassador came to see me several times to repeat Saddam's offer and to try to resolve our border problems. I warned him, "After what Khomeini experienced in your country, don't expect gratitude; you should be aware, however, that I am against this escalation between our two countries. I must ask you not to give Khomeini any pretext by helping the Kurds and the other opposition groups."

Unfortunately, my successor, Ghotbzadeh, followed Khomeini's lead and added fuel to the fire of our relations with the Iraqis, thus hastening a war that we knew was inevitable.

6

A GENERALLY
EXPEDIENT WAR

SIGNS HERALDING THE IRAQI ASSAULT APPEARED IN EVER
increasing numbers. In addition to the troop concentrations and
the provocations in the field, the Iraqis had begun persecuting the
ulama of Najaf. They even arrested and executed Ayatollah
Mohammed Bagher Sadr, a highly respected progressive intellectual. The Iraqis categorically rejected the possibility of a Shiite-
Sunni clash within their borders, although the danger of an
uprising uniting Iraqi Kurds, Iraqi Shiites, and even Sunnis
opposed to the Baathist regime was very real. Saddam Hussein,
however, did not hesitate to transform our border disputes into
a religious war in order to portray Iranian Islam to the Iraqi public
as an abomination.

In the archives of our army's second bureau, in a department
headed by the Americans during the Shah's reign, we found a plan
for restoring the monarchy. As a member of the Revolutionary
Council, I had been appointed to head an investigation into
"leaks" to the Soviet Union. It was thus more or less by chance
that the investigators happened upon this document, which, in
the event of a revolution, called for preserving the existing
structures—especially the administrative, banking, and budget-

ary structures—and maintaining oil sales at a level of six million barrels a day, the purpose being not only to sustain the national economy but also to keep Iran dependent on foreign powers until the revolutionary fervor subsided. Much of the plan concerned the army, which was to be preserved through the creation of internal and external threats. The internal threat—civil disturbances in the provinces—was clearly identified. The external threat was not specified, but the only logical choice was a hostile neighbor. We had only one.

This document largely explains the course of events to date. It was obvious at the time that relations had been established between Iraq and the United States. History cannot be rewritten, but I cannot help thinking that if Khomeini had not refused his offer of friendship, Saddam might not have cooperated with the Americans. The Imam, who knew nothing about international politics, had only one idea in his head: overthrowing the Iraqi regime that had persecuted him.

One day I heard on the radio that Khomeini had just named me commander in chief of the army. This delegation of power was not due exclusively to his declining health, although his physician did expect the worst. Ever since the revolution, the army had been disorganized and the soldiers and officers had regularly gone on strike. Khomeini therefore wanted to put me up against the military to prove that I was incapable of controlling the situation, which seemed more than likely since my predecessors in this position had all failed. The mullahs said repeatedly that this army of the Shah's was useless, that it had chosen inertia as a means of subverting the revolution.

Immediately after my appointment, I organized meetings with the officers to explain the situation to them. "If you think you can bring the mullahs to their knees with your disorganization, you are mistaken. They appointed me—wanting me to fail—in order to destroy me as well as you. The field will then be open; you will be replaced by the Revolutionary Guards, I by a mullah." They understood this language very clearly.

The internal disturbances called for in the American plan began at this time. The army chief of staff informed me one day that elementary and high school students in Sanandaj, the capital of Kurdistan, had occupied the city's airport to prevent the

•

soldiers from reaching their barracks. However, Abod-elrahaman Gassemlou, leader of the PDKI, had recently sent an envoy to Tehran, and we had agreed that his organization would prevent any disturbances and provocations orchestrated by outsiders. Extremely surprised, I had my advisers contact Gassemlou. He denied responsibility for this demonstration and blamed it on the Komoleh, a rival pro-Communist organization. I inferred from this that Iraq was not far off. Eric Rouleau, a French journalist specially assigned to Tehran, met with Gassemlou and then went to Baghdad. In an article in *Le Monde*, Rouleau expressed his conviction that Baghdad was manipulating the Kurds and that their demands for autonomy were merely a pretext.

After this student demonstration, we quickly put down the resistance with a minimum of damages. Many of the documents we confiscated concerned Iraq, which had assigned men to the Kurdish organizations to oversee the use of funds. One of the documents called for the distribution of munitions from the Sanandaj garrison once the Iranian army was defeated.

IRAQI THREATS

No sooner had we solved our internal problems in Kurdistan, Khuzestan, and West Azerbaijan, where a group was sabotaging the railroad, than Saddam Hussein stepped in to take their place.

The Iraqis were making increasingly specific threats, claiming that Iran could not withstand an attack for long because its air force was nonexistent. I asked a group of experts to prepare a report on the state of the armed forces, which proved to be alarming since the army had a combat capability of zero, the navy 10 percent, and the air force 20 percent. The Iraqis were not far off the mark and had they attacked then, would have had every chance of a rapid victory. But they had not received the green light from the United States. This six-month respite gave us time to reorganize our army.

With the threats becoming more and more explicit, I gave Yasser Arafat a message for Saddam Hussein, the text of which I still have: "You imagine that you can finish Iran with a lightning war because our army is disorganized. You dream of becoming

•

the pre-eminent power in the region. This is all the work of your imagination. You can start a war, but you cannot decide its outcome. Why make the whole world a witness of our stupidity? If you start a war, you will be playing into the mullahs' hands and they will establish a religious dictatorship. If you want to prevent that, why this war?"

Yasser Arafat made the trip to Baghdad and then came back to report on his meeting with Saddam Hussein, who had peremptorily informed him, "Do not concern yourself about that. It will last only a few days; it will be a simple exercise. The Palestinians will be the first to benefit from this war because a victory this quick will frighten the Israelis."

Just as Khomeini was certain that no one would attack Iran, Saddam was sure that the war would be a simple exercise. Who put these ideas into their heads?

We knew that Zbigniew Brzezinski, Carter's national security adviser, and Saddam Hussein had met in the first week of July 1980. Brzezinski has never denied this trip to Amman and in his autobiography* refers to the Iran-Iraq war once, saying that he prepared a report for Carter explaining that this conflict was consistent with American policy in the region.

During this same month, the Soviet ambassador came to advise me that his country had informed the Iraqis of its opposition to an attack on Iran. The information was confirmed by the Algerian ambassador, who also told me that the Soviets refused to deliver arms to them. During this visit, the Soviet ambassador also pointed out that his country's relations with Iraq had cooled. He could hardly have been more specific. "Saddam Hussein is now in the same situation Sadat was in before he went to Jerusalem; in other words, he is going to fall into the American camp." To me, this meant war, pure and simple.

Khomeini pretended not to believe it. He kept telling anyone who would listen, "No one would dare attack Iran; this is a maneuver on the part of the officers to escape the mullahs' control." We knew, however, that following their victory, the Iraqis planned to divide Iran into five republics to finish us as a

---

* *Power and Principle: Memoirs of the National Security Adviser, 1977-1981* (New York: Farrar, Straus & Giroux, 1983), pp. 568-69.

•

regional power once and for all. The antirevolutionaries Bakhtiar and General Gholam Oveissi were unaware of Saddam Hussein's true intentions when they went to Baghdad to negotiate a plan to overthrow the Iranian regime. It was agreed that they, with Iraqi assistance, would occupy the oil-producing regions in western Iran, establish a government there, and then liberate the rest of the country.

Convinced of the inevitability of this war, I used the precious time remaining to us to reorganize our army. We had three divisions tied up in Iranian Kurdistan while the one in Khuzestan was leaderless because of the purges, and we had discovered eight conspiracies in the other divisions.

Only our air force and navy were functioning properly, and this was because they had escaped the mullahs' control. Khomeini always said about the air force, "Up there, a coup is impossible."

These military coup attempts were the opportunity the mullahs had been dreaming of to eliminate the army and replace it with the revolutionary organizations. They chose three methods to achieve their goals: turning public opinion against the army, disorganizing it from within, and militating for a guerrilla war that the Revolutionary Guards could lead without the support of the regular army.

Khomeini, who officially rejected the possibility of a war, was well aware of the danger and intervened between the mullahs and the army to limit the purges somewhat. He also publicly renewed his confidence in me as commander in chief of the armed forces.

I introduced a slogan: "Let's apply freedom in the army." In fact, a study had revealed to me that our officers, noncommissioned officers, and soldiers lived under a system of forty-eight unjust and inexplicable advantages and prerogatives inherited from the Shah, which I abolished. The concentration of power in the commander in chief had been farcical. For a soldier to be granted leave, it was almost necessary to obtain the Shah's signature! The most pressing reforms consisted of dividing responsibilities and giving each individual the necessary degree of authority, from the top of the chain of command to the bottom.

We agreed that we would view the army as a great university, meaning that anyone who entered as a soldier might leave as a general.   During the Shah's reign, when the class system prevailed, a person entered the army a soldier and left a soldier. In these circumstances, authority was exercised by incompetents with only one positive trait: obedience.   The purpose of democratizing the army was to replace all these classes and the various levels of incompetents placed over them.   This was the beginning of a military reform that I wanted to continue.

Confident of Khomeini's neutrality, if not his support, I even managed to organize a rout of the mullahs who had invaded the barracks.   Stick-wielding soldiers drove them out.   These initial measures helped to boost the morale of the army, which would soon be called upon to counter the Iraqi offensive.

Skirmishes on the front became daily occurrences.   With Prime Minister Rajai, we went to Kermanshah to determine the status of our forces.   Our military leaders told us at once that they believed themselves capable of resisting an attack for four days. We had made efforts, but the overall picture was still disastrous since only twenty-seven Chieftain tanks out of 160 were in working order, 270 officers from the Khuzestan division were in prison, and the rest of our forces were actively engaged in Kurdistan.

I gave them as much encouragement as I could, and I related our conversation to Khomeini, who recognized the gravity of the situation.   He finally understood that if we were defeated in four days, it would be the end not only of Iran but of himself as well. His hands began to tremble.   He was frightened.

7

BETWEEN FEAR AND HOPE

The Iraqi Attack

THE THING WE DREADED OCCURRED ON SEPTEMBER 22. Iraq's ground and air forces began the lightning war envisioned by Saddam Hussein. Within a matter of hours, tanks crossed our borders at several points and our air bases were bombed. This classic, Dayan-style strategy—which consists of pinning the enemy's air force to the ground to prevent a reprisal—failed because we had advance information and had moved our planes to safety; only the buildings were damaged. We immediately decided to retaliate by air to prove to the Iraqis the failure of their strategy and to slow the advance on the ground. However, we delayed these air strikes for several hours, because I wanted to give Algerian president Chadli Benjelid time to reason with Saddam Hussein while it was still possible to limit the damage.

We destroyed several enemy bases, but the situation was far from encouraging because, with our army in a state of ruin, Saddam Hussein had almost free rein on the ground.

The day after the attack, I went to see Khomeini to read him the speech I planned to give on television. I minced no words and held back nothing concerning the situation and the difficulties in store for us. At the end of my speech, I noticed that he was deathly pale and that his hands were shaking. I realized that if I gave this speech, panic might make him say things that would completely demoralize the people and the army. On leaving, I decided to change the tone, to make a show of optimism to prevent general panic.

I remained at the armed forces general staff headquarters in Tehran day and night. The room had been equipped by the Americans during the Shah's reign. Multicolored electronic maps showed the progress of the armies. It was possible, simply by pushing a button, to observe the position of any Iraqi division. According to these maps we were in good shape, but this was unfortunately far from true. I found myself in a paradoxical and dangerous situation. I was the first elected president of a people who had fought a revolution against the army, and I was living at general staff headquarters! The risk was increased by the fact that we had exposed a number of plots, but I had to take that risk to make the military understand that it was now or never as far as becoming a national army was concerned.

In the first two days everyone panicked. Khomeini, Beheshti, and Rafsanjani all believed that we would be defeated. One after the other, they came to assure me of their support and to say that our quarrels were forgotten. It was not in their interest for Iraq to win a lightning war, because they would be swept away. I took advantage of the confusion in their ranks to do things my way. By mid-October, when they felt reassured, their attitude was completely different.

Since the army, by its own admission, could only hold out for four days, the Revolutionary Guards and Rajai resurrected their guerrilla idea. The defeated regular army would be eliminated, and the Guards would step in to conduct the war their way. They had even sent a report on this subject to Khomeini.

In a general staff meeting, I asked the commander of the Revolutionary Guards two questions: "If the army were abolished, could you conduct this guerrilla war alone? Also, do you yourselves have the means to hold Kurdistan and Azerbaijan while the army fights the war?" They answered no to both of these questions. I concluded that it was impossible to abolish the regular army in the current circumstances because the Iraqis would only have to occupy Khuzestan, Iran's leading oil-producing region, for the country to cease to exist. I asked the commander one last question: "How could you quickly mobilize the people for a guerrilla war?" No response. Thus, everyone at the meeting understood, as I did, that guerrilla warfare was feasible only in case of total defeat.

In the first few days of the war, I met with all of the leaders of the army to put things into focus. "Defeated by Iraq, Iran will have a slight chance of survival, but you will have none. The people have already fought a revolution against you and your reconciliation with the people is still incomplete. If, in addition, you sustain a military defeat, you are doomed. You have no choice; you must stand and die in the fight to save your country, your honor, and perhaps your army, for no one will be able to challenge you if you succeed. The plan to replace you with the Guards will be forgotten." This sudden awareness on the part of the military leaders was to change many things at the beginning of the war.

Khomeini astonished me one day as I was extolling the merits of our army, which was somehow managing to resist the enemy. He interrupted me to say, "Do not forget that this army was created with the idea of the Shah as the symbol of God, the country personified. The Shah is in their blood; the Guards, on the other hand, even if they sometimes go too far, have Islam in their blood." I answered, "No, you are wrong to distrust the army, which now obeys an authority legitimized not only by the revolution but by the way the Shah fled abroad. They realize that the Americans 'tossed him out like a dead mouse.' For both these reasons, this army is less dangerous than your Guards, who think they have license to do anything because they call themselves 'guardians of the Islamic revolution.' They see themselves as protectors of the new regime. They use power as if it were their personal property. You should distrust them instead."

Immediately after this meeting, Khomeini's son Ahmed asked me to visit the army warehouses. For one whole day we toured the storage depots and noted that many things were lacking. If we had had the necessary equipment, we could have halted the Iraqi aggression immediately. As it was, we had to adapt our tactics to these shortages.

Despite this handicap, the Iraqi tanks were brought to a

·

standstill after four days because our ground forces, backed by the air force, were increasingly successful in slowing their advance.

Time was on our side. Already, Saddam Hussein could no longer speak of a lightning victory.

The war immediately became a source of contention within the regime. I was afraid the conflict would go on forever since Rajai, the head of government, told anyone who would listen, "This war is a blessing from God; let's hope it lasts a year or more." In the midst of war, with the enemy on our territory, the mullahs even dared to say that losing half of Iran would be better than a Bani-Sadr victory.

Worst of all, Khomeini made the government's position his own by declaring that the war was a blessing. How can a religious leader make such remarks? The Koran is very clear: War is the work of Satan.

For me, continuing the war meant ultimately "bringing it home," as in Lebanon, where the loss of property and often of life itself are a part of each family's daily experience. Up to the ceasefire in 1988, and despite the missiles fired on the cities, whole regions escaped destruction. It is not that the mullahs are less cruel than Saddam Hussein—they would be even more so— but the people instinctively refuse to "interiorize" wars. The historic experience of the Iranian people is responsible for this phenomenon. Every time war was interiorized, massacres followed. Between the close of the Safavid era and the advent of the Kajars, thirty years of internal warfare reduced the Iranian population from 40 to 10 million. Historic memory is extremely powerful and sharpens the people's vigilance. We wanted to prevent interiorization of the war. The mullahs—anxious to strengthen the revolutionary organizations, committees, and tribunals—wanted just the opposite.

On September 25, I received a visit from the Algerian ambassador, who offered me the mediation services of President Chadli Benjelid and the Emir of Kuwait.

He insisted on three points. First, the Iraqis had been pushed into the war by the Americans (I already knew that). Second, the solution of the crisis lay in the hostage affair, and finally, what was most interesting, the Arabs had quickly realized that Saddam Hussein had lost all chances of a rapid victory. I related this conversation to Khomeini's son so that he would know that the Arab countries considered us the winners. It was very encouraging for us. I urged the ambassador to ask Benjelid to exert greater pressure on Saddam Hussein to stop the war because I knew that its continuation would aggravate our internal problems.

THE POTENTIAL PEACE

On September 26, Zia ul-Haq, then president of neighboring Pakistan, and Habib Chatti, secretary general of the Islamic Conference, came to see me. As Muslims, we discussed Islamic principles. The Koran teaches that in case of war between two Muslim countries, believers must ally themselves with whomever has right on his side and force peace on the other. Right was on our side since we were attacked without provocation. To accept a compromise advantageous to the aggressor was inconceivable. Zia ul-Haq said that in my place he would feel the same way. The next day, Arafat joined us. He explained the devastating effects this war was having on the Palestinians since Israel could take advantage of the situation to annihilate them. His analysis proved to be prophetic. Two years later, Israel invaded Lebanon in pursuit of Palestinians. He added, "You must realize that the world would not allow you to go all the way to Baghdad, nor would it allow the Iraqis into Tehran. You should therefore accept the immediate ceasefire which Saddam Hussein is offering you through me." We then analyzed the impact of the conflict on the region and concluded that its continuation would weaken the position of Syria and the Palestinians in western Iran and would aggravate the situation in Pakistan and Soviet-occupied Afghanistan. We all agreed that the best solution was immediate peace, on the condition that Iraq, as I demanded, first accept a return to the border, then a ceasefire, and not the other way around, as Saddam Hussein had just suggested. My counteroffer could be summed up in one sentence: return to the border, then a ceasefire and a promise not to interfere in Iran's affairs.

Ahmed Khomeini came to see me the same day. I had asked him to come so that he could tell his father what I had said in these discussions. I still had full confidence in Khomeini. I did not know that all his thinking was about to change because the fear of defeat was receding and being replaced by the fear of a victory not advantageous to himself. The possibility of a victory suddenly became a problem for him. The credit would go to Bani-Sadr, who, with a disorganized army, would have routed an invading force that had been trained for twelve years and was considered to be the best in the Middle East. Without knowing it, I became a potential threat to Khomeini from that moment on.

Nevertheless, the situation was not so good. We still could not rule out an Iraqi victory because the progress of the fighting remained a source of concern. When Khomeini received me on September 28, he was unusually obstinate and was now demanding Saddam's head. I could not keep from laughing. "A week ago, everyone was afraid that Iran was going to lose and now you are demanding Saddam Hussein's resignation. A Chinese proverb says, 'When you win, do not spend everything.'" I explained to Khomeini that we should accept the peace because it would be a victory for the spirit of the Iranian revolution and the Iraqi defeat would show the people of the Third World that the armies dominating them are not invincible. Above all, we did not have the means to continue fighting a futile war. If we imposed peace in a few days, as was conceivable, the Iraqi regime would never recover. The fall of this dictatorship would serve as an example to the Muslim countries. For all of these reasons, I was convinced that the war would end soon. This is also what I told Eric Rouleau of *Le Monde* in an interview.

The conflict was prolonged because there was an imperative internal necessity for doing so.

Consider, for a moment, the following scenario. Imagine the hostage problem solved and Bani-Sadr victorious. The mullahs would be prevented from imposing the dictatorship they had erected stone by stone.

Officially, Khomeini had no choice but to accept the peace proposals I was offering him, but this did not prevent him from immediately starting to work in the opposite direction. It must be admitted that Saddam Hussein failed to seize the opportunity.

The day after this meeting with the Imam, a messenger from Rafsanjani, Mohammed Javad Bahonar, and Beheshti came to propose a reconciliation. I showed him the door, because this

•

was not the first time they had tried this with me. When the situation in the field was bad, they were extremely conciliatory and urged me to compromise, but the next day, if the situation improved, they became champions of all-out war. I knew perfectly well what they were doing. In the early days of the war, they were for a ceasefire at any price because it would have meant defeat for Bani-Sadr. Eight days later, they attacked the prospective truce in their newspapers. My first suspicions about Khomeini began at this time. How did these mullahs know about the counterproposals I had made to Yasser Arafat if Khomeini did not tell them?

A PRECARIOUS SITUATION

On September 27, however, there was no room for optimism. We had received a series of disturbing reports. Two of the reports were submitted by Ghotbzadeh, who was very well-informed. One concerned the royalist groups hired by the Iraqis to establish a puppet regime in Iran if the Iraqis won; the other was a list of collaborators within the regime, a fifth column in the leadership of the Islamic Republic Party, which was working to prevent an Iranian victory. A third, equally troubling report warned us that the Americans were about to take action to force us to release the hostages. At the time, we had no details concerning this plan; we imagined an attack on our ports or airports. What I am saying here is corroborated by documents I have in my possession.

Finally, on this same day, I received a telephone report that Desfoul, the most important city in Khuzestan, was on the point of falling. I left Tehran immediately for the front, where we landed in the midst of the bombing. A pilot I knew approached me immediately. "They are hiding the truth from you; our ground forces are nonexistent. The highway is open; the Iraqis can be in Desfoul in two hours. The base is going to fall into their hands."

I met with the pilots, and we decided to hold the Iraqis on the other side of the Karkheh River at all costs.

For a week, they held off an entire division by intensifying the air raids. We used this respite to regroup our ground forces and to take a strategic position that enabled us to save Khuzestan.

•

Again, I called together all the army officers to inform them that I would be staying with them on the front and to renew my order to rid the barracks and bases of all mullahs.

On October 2, I went to see Khomeini. He was smiling. "You, an intellectual who has written against war, could you ever have imagined that you would one day lead an army in combat?"

"No," I answered, "but I am learning to hate war more than ever." I recalled a Persian poem by Nasser Khosrow, in which a proud, self-important eagle is flying in the sky when he is suddenly pierced by an arrow. In his fall, he notices that the arrow passing through his body is made of eagle feathers and with his last breath says, "My death is of my own making." We are in the same situation. The war is of our own making, and that is what bothers me the most. Khomeini listened closely.

"I have often warned you. We could have stopped the war in time, but you never listened to me. Let's stop it now. You know that much more is at stake than the conflict with Saddam and that the superpowers of this world cannot stand the thought of an independent Iran because it would set a bad example for neighboring countries."

I proposed a three-point plan for unifying our regime. First, I asked that all responsibility for conducting the war be concentrated in the Military Council and that all other authorities be prohibited from interfering because war is the business of strategists, not mullahs. Second, I asked that internal and external propaganda, as well as Iran's foreign policy, be determined by the Supreme Defense Council, which comprises all of the highest authorities of the country. Third, I asked that Khomeini forbid the Islamic Republic Party to conduct a war of political propaganda within the regime.

He told me that he would think about these proposals and asked me to send him a written draft, which I wrote immediately.

At this time, the people were following their leaders and their commitment was total: in a single day, 80,000 reservists signed up. This was a great many more than we could actually handle.

On October 2, Zia ul-Haq sent me Iraq's response. Saddam Hussein's position was unchanged. He wanted a ceasefire before returning to the border, with the proviso that we accept his denunciation of the Algiers Agreement of 1975, which had placed the border between our two countries in the middle of the Shatt-al-Arab waterway. This position, which was unacceptable to us, meant that Iraq was going Khomeini one better and wanted to continue the conflict. Khomeini immediately became afraid. He told himself that if Saddam Hussein were so demanding, it was because he was strong or had received assurances. The rumor of an American attack resurfaced.

This second wave of fear lasted from October 3 to October 8. Like the first time, I took advantage of it and on October 4 signed the decree democratizing the army.

Fear had an immediate impact on Khomeini, who unconditionally approved the three-point plan I had submitted to him. At this time, he favored an end to the hostilities and was supported in this view of things by the Supreme Judicial Council, whose five members—Beheshti, Ardebili, and three other mullahs—traveled all the way to army headquarters to assure me of their support.

The first month of the war ended with us wavering between fear and hope.

8

WAR

A Blessing for the Mullahs

OCTOBER 10, 1980, IS AN IMPORTANT DATE BECAUSE THE Iraqi army was at a standstill. Except for the siege of Khorramshahr, the attacks were no longer significant.

Khomeini, giving in to pressure from the mullahs, issued a decree creating a new defense council including the head of parliament (Rafsanjani) and two deputies appointed by him. My isolation not being sufficient for Rafsanjani, he also wanted to prevent me from presiding over this new council, the existence of which had no basis in the Constitution. Seeing my anger, he backed down and proposed my immediate election to the chairmanship, which I also refused since, according to the Constitution, I am the lawful chairman of the Supreme Defense Council. I boycotted this new authority and then managed quietly to dissolve it after only two or three meetings.

When it seemed obvious that Iraq would not win the war, the disturbances in Kurdistan and West Azerbaijan resumed. This was not particularly troubling, but I realized that the mullahs were trying to create a new front by inciting the tribes and their political organizations to revolt. The Guards and the *hezbollah* (party of

God) were provoking the tribes, who naturally retaliated by attacking us.

On October 11, just after we had repulsed the Iraqi army at Abadan, I received a visit from Montazeri and Taheri, the Imam of Friday prayers in Isfahan. I explained to them in detail the danger that the antagonism between the Guards and the army represented for the country. I called in several division commanders who told of the cruel treatment they had suffered at the hands of the Revolutionary Guards—beatings, burns, and such. Montazeri then offered me his support, which I accepted. "Watch the home front. Stop the spread of internal, psychological, political, military, and economic warfare. Tell these mullahs that in case of defeat, they will be the first victims."

Montazeri soon changed his position. His son Mohamad, the sworn enemy of Beheshti, whom he considered a representative of the American line, came one day to ask me to spare Beheshti and his friends. This about-face surprised me, because I had not realized that the purpose of all his attacks had been to obtain a seat in the Assembly. His coming to see me meant that he now wanted to climb higher. Without any hesitation, he asked me to make him commander of the Revolutionary Guards or foreign affairs minister. My refusal caused the change in his father's attitude, and I made myself one more enemy. . . .

For the first time, on October 13, we launched an attack ourselves, but without great success. Despite considerable loss of life, this offensive marked a change in the psychological scheme of things: we were now able to initiate attacks.

That same evening, in the general staff meeting, the officers agreed that they had hurried the offensive under pressure from the mullahs. They also blamed this failure on the lack of information. We decided to reorganize the services disbanded during the revolution. We created sections in charge of analyzing the press, listening to the radio, and recording Iraqi television news programs. We bought sophisticated listening equipment and organized the systematic questioning of prisoners to obtain useful information.

Thus, we were able to analyze very precisely the political, military, and economic situation in Iraq on a day-to-day basis. We learned, for example, that Saddam Hussein was afraid of large-scale operations and that he always held back part of his forces. He failed to realize that a massive offensive would have brought us to our knees immediately. We also observed that the very tight control he exercised over the military command paralyzed it; the military leaders never dared to question his instructions. We quickly took advantage of these weaknesses and made up for our lack of resources by amassing information in all sectors.

Several experts studied the behavior of Saddam Hussein himself. They read all his speeches and recorded all his television interviews. The face reveals the inner workings of the mind. Khomeini, in his lifetime, was the best source of information about the Iranian regime. I studied everything he said, word by word. I knew him so well that I could tell what state of mind he was in by reading between the lines of his speeches.

Unfortunately, information is not enough to win a war. Without equipment, spare parts, maintenance, or logistics, no army in the world can hold out for very long. The lack of spare parts was our major handicap. We therefore undertook the transformation of certain industries. A genuine metamorphosis took place in some sectors. Shops that ordinarily took two weeks to repair a motor were putting two in working order every day. The whole country was at war.

Our first success was in halting the Iraqi army. Our objective after three weeks of combat was to end the occupation. Two options were available to us: stopping at the border or pursuit into enemy territory.

Certain officers suggested acting quickly. Accepting the ceasefire immediately would allow us to regroup before liberating our territory once and for all.

No one wanted to cross the border because we lacked the resources. I thought that the ceasefire should not be accepted with the Iraqis still on our territory because the mullahs could weaken the army while it was tied up on the front and form their own contingent of Guards behind the lines, which would replace the military. Consequently, we decided that the war would end at the border. In full agreement with the military, I gave the people a new battle cry: "We on the front are fighting the Iraqis, and you, the people, must combat the dictatorial tendencies at home." My supporters went from city to city to speak about the monopolization of power by the mullahs.

Instead of allowing unofficial units to form outside the army, we decided that the army would itself organize new units to prevent two, three, or four armies from fighting the war, as in Lebanon.

Ever since my arrival at the front, I had been unable to accept the idea that we were expending so much effort to prepare for the death of our soldiers. Every time I visited the pilots, I told myself that I might be seeing them for the last time. Even their families were in danger since they lived with them on the base. One of my first decisions was to evacuate the families to Tehran. The soldiers constantly insisted that I stay in the army staff headquarters in an underground bunker. They always told me the same thing, "What would the people say if the president died on our base? They would accuse us of murder. Since the army is already suspected of treason, we are taking too many risks by keeping you here."

I was never able to convince myself to follow their advice. The air force bore the brunt of the war, and had I lived underground, I would not have had the courage to face these pilots who were risking their lives on every single raid.

Then the Iraqis began attacking the cities. The first missile fell in Desfoul. We were sure that it was a mistake and that they were aiming at the air base where I was. I went to see the damage and, for the first time, I heard the people cry, "Down with Khomeini!" It astounded me. The people realized that the country was beginning to pay a heavy price for the mullahs' push for dictatorship. The crowd shouted, "Down with the three crooks—Behehsti, Khamenei, Rafsanjani!" and "Bani-Sadr, missile for missile!" Khamenei, now "Guide" of the Republic, was scheduled to give a speech at the mosque that afternoon. I decided to go. The slogan "Missile for missile" resounded through the vaults of the mosque. I got up to calm the crowd.

"Do you think it fair for Saddam Hussein to attack you with missiles? No? Then why do you want us to do the same thing to the people of Iraq, our neighbors with whom we will be living in the years to come? We are a civilized nation and I refuse to let

•

history record that I, your first elected leader, ordered the same crimes as a dictator. Even if I had the missiles, I would not fight crime with crime. Shall we live in friendship with these Arabs from the other side of the river, or in hostility under American and Soviet domination? They must understand that there is a difference between a democratic, fraternal Islam and a cruel, lawless fascism. That is where our strength lies, our most effective weapon against this barbaric dictatorship."

The reaction was extraordinary because, for once, violence did not sway the masses; aggression was put down.

THE MULLAHS VERSUS THE ARMY

The demoralization of the army in this period came not from the enemy, but from our own ranks. The pilots, whom I considered the saviors of Iran, were the mullahs' favorite target. In a meeting on the Desfoul air base, one of the pilots asked me to read the interview of a deputy in the Islamic Republic Party newspaper who blasted specialists and technicians, all of whom were servants of the Americans. This pilot's anger was understandable. "This is how we are repaid! You say that we are Iran's saviors and parliament treats us like CIA agents!" How could these pilots, who were risking their lives every day, help but feel demoralized? It would have been difficult for me to admit to them that they were going to die so that the mullahs could govern their country.

It was for this basic reason that the army was never able to reconcile itself with the mullahs. Relations between the army and the Islamic Republic Party had deteriorated to such an extent that when the soldiers wanted to insult someone, they called him an "IRP" organizer.

As the elected president of this people, I realized that I could no longer differentiate between my own son or daughter and the other young Iranians who were fighting. One day I was shown the charred body of a young student whose mother had made him return from England to defend his country. What could I say to the woman? I wrote to her as though it had been my own son. On another occasion, I slept in a village at the home of a noncommissioned officer whose wife slipped a letter under my pillow. "Mr. President, welcome. We trust you. It is an honor for us to serve our country under your command." My position was untenable. I was caught between outside forces seeking to crush our revolution at all costs, and the mullahs, who wanted to impose a dictatorship. Telling the people the truth would have forced Khomeini and the others to attack us. Keeping silent meant betraying the confidence of these people. I often felt the desire to throw off this burden, which was very heavy to bear. For this reason also, I wanted to get the war over very quickly.

On October 26, deputy Hassan Ayyat said in an interview in an Italian newspaper that this would be a long war, that in the course of it the army would be disbanded and replaced by the Revolutionary Guards, and that the conflict could spread throughout the region. These remarks had no other purpose than to demoralize the army, stir up opposition (because he knew I would react), and induce the Iraqis to continue the war.

I became increasingly convinced that these mullahs did not want a military victory. Did Khomeini think like them? I was never able to give a definite answer to that question. He said one day that the army was treasonous and on the next assured it of his confidence. In fact, when he sent Ardebili to tell me that there were reports accusing the army of treason, it was an Iranian-style message, that is, coded. He wanted to let me know that I should not link my fate too closely to the military. Khomeini constantly circulated such rumors, which he knew to be false, just to make sure that the arms delivered went to the Guards and not the regular army. He also talked about a military coup d'état, failing to realize that coups are not organized by popular armies, but by those that are despised. The Iranian army had become very popular. We stressed the importance of the officers' work, and we respected the soldiers so that they, in turn, would respect democracy. I told Khomeini's son, so that he could repeat it to his father, "Don't be afraid of a military victory; fear defeat instead. With a victory, the soldiers will not do anything foolish. However, if they are defeated, they will blame you and then the risk of a coup will be real."

On the front, the Revolutionary Guards stepped up their provocations. I was constantly forced to act as a referee to prevent clashes with the soldiers. They avoided opposing the army

•

directly, preferring instead to short-circuit our plans by attacking the enemy unexpectedly or else trying to appropriate weapons delivered to the front.

The defeat we suffered between October 17 and October 20 symbolizes for me the disorganization of our defense system. Fifteen armed groups were defending Khorramshahr, guerrilla style. This experience is indicative of how the mullahs viewed the war. For the first time, I blamed Khomeini himself. How could fifteen groups have taken up positions without the approval of the commander in chief of the armed forces? Who had given them authorization if not Khomeini himself, who wanted to satisfy the revolutionary organizations?

We very quickly realized that the western section of the city was going to fall. It was then that a member of the Imam's staff telephoned me to say that if Khorramshahr fell, Khomeini could no longer support me as commander in chief. I was furious. "I am not responsible for the defense of that city, so why are you threatening me?" Khomeini knew very well that I had no authority over the fifteen groups defending Khorramshahr without regard for the directives of the military command. Instead of abandoning this stupid guerrilla tactic, he wanted me to shoulder the responsibility for a defeat.

This anarchy in the conduct of the war had to stop, so I threatened Khomeini by telling his son I was going to tell everything I knew. Grudgingly, he assured me of his support.

The offensive against me escalated. The mullahs took advantage of the occupation of Khorramshahr to have a petition signed by about a hundred deputies demanding my removal as commander in chief of the armed forces. This defeat—entirely attributable to the mullahs—was not a catastrophe; however, the city was not strategically important and the task of surrounding it had immobilized a large segment of the Iraqi army, enabling us to deploy our troops to other locations on the front. The public understood clearly what the mullahs were up to and expressed its support for my policy, backed by a hundred or so other deputies who signed a petition in my favor.

The war with Iraq was becoming secondary; the real war was now going on within the regime.

The Supreme Judicial Council entered the fray. It passed a

•

number of very restrictive laws providing punishments for anyone who violated military regulations, the curfew, and censorship, in particular. The Council viewed the war as an opportunity to restrict freedoms. I protested constantly against the clerical judges who were being sent to the barracks to demoralize the army. I no longer hesitated to speak openly of the fifth column that was sabotaging the soldiers' efforts.

On November 7, we concluded that the Iraqi army could neither advance nor retreat. This was the moment to end the war, but Beheshti and his aides disagreed. They had invented a new slogan: "Even if this war lasts twenty years, we are ready."

They constantly disparaged the army's work and the expertise of our technicians and advocated guerrilla warfare. Our revolution succeeded without guerrilla combat, unlike all the other revolutions fought during the same period; nevertheless, there were organizations in Iran capable of fighting this type of war. We had chosen another method that prevented any one organization from taking control of the revolution. No holds were barred as far as harassing the army was concerned. One day, the commander in chief of our ground forces was arrested by a Basij who asked for his papers and detained him, despite his protests. I had to send my guards to obtain his release. How could anyone conduct a war in such conditions?

Despite everything, the Supreme Defense Council was forced to admit that the army's state of mind had changed. It also had to recognize that the balance of forces between us and the Iraqis was shifting. The mullahs' attitude had not changed. On the contrary, they were strengthened in their conviction that the army had to be eliminated as quickly as possible.

On November 16, for the first time, we liberated an occupied city, Sousanguerd. The Iraqis lost scores of men and equipment. We took prisoners as young as fifteen and sixteen years of age. Contrary to what has been said, it was the Iraqis who began using children in the war. This I found utterly astonishing, but I learned from reading the transcripts of interrogations that they were not involved in guerrilla warfare, as the mullahs claimed, but were sent to the front to create the illusion of numbers.

Starting also on this date, the number of Iraqi dead and prisoners increased considerably. We attached great importance to the human factor, which was the Iraqi army's weak point. At this time, there were not a million Egyptians working in Iraq. If we could neutralize the Iraqi military experts, we would win.

The Iraqi army was stalled on a vast open plain without natural cover and our soldiers were firing on the enemy as though on a hunting expedition. This was a problem for me. I gave it considerable thought and then gave the order to limit the number of deaths. These soldiers were people who were being manipulated or forced to do what they were doing. We looked for ways of achieving results militarily with a minimum of deaths on either side. Until then, I had been receiving nightly statistical reports on Iraqi losses. I could no longer stand this morbid accounting. I ordered it stopped. During the offensive in the "Allah O Akbar" mountains in Khuzestan, we succeeded in limiting the losses: three hundred Iraqi dead, twenty-four on our side. We took a great many prisoners, however, which created a new problem. What were we to do with these men, and how were we to treat them? I knew that the mullahs were interested in the prisoners since Hakim was in Iran. Hakim is a Shiite Iraqi dissident who had joined our ranks. He wanted to organize an army using the prisoners of war. I categorically refused to permit this and insisted at all times that the regular army and no one else guard the prisoners in order to ensure their safety and prevent abuses. I had absolutely no confidence in Hakim, who had suggested to me that we bomb Iraqi cities. He claimed that if we bombed the cities, the people would revolt against the Baathist regime. I was convinced of the reverse; the people, having lost everything, would be more subjugated than ever.

Militarily, then, after two months of war, we were in a position to impose a peace advantageous to Iran. During this period, there was a flurry of diplomatic activity.

9

ENTER THE SUPERPOWERS

SINCE THE BEGINNING OF THE WAR, I HAD BEEN ANALYZING the positions of the Americans and the Soviets, who surely never imagined such a capacity for resistance on our part. I thought that the Carter administration, anxious for the hostages' release, would help me win the peace even though my strategy was incompatible with American interests in the Middle East, which are always threatened by a peaceful revolution.

Unexpected proof of Carter's goodwill arrived on October 7, 1980. I had invited the Swiss ambassador to Tehran that day to ask him to deliver a protest to the Americans concerning the information that the American AWACS (airborne warning and control system) aircraft sold to Saudi Arabia would be at the disposal of the Iraqis. The Swiss ambassador returned the next day with a two-part message. President Carter assured us that his AWACS would provide the Iraqis with no information and insisted that if the Iraqis did get any information, it would be from the Soviets. I never knew if what he said was true; there was no way of checking it. The second part of Carter's message was of vital importance. He assured me that, for geopolitical reasons, the United States would never accept Iran's defeat. He even suggested providing us with all the arms we wanted if we would quickly resolve the hostage problem.

Europe and Japan did not look favorably on a continuation of the war because their economies were heavily dependent on the region's oil. A prolonged conflict would mean cheaper oil, but also the risk of an interruption in supply. European influence at the time tended more toward peace than war.

The Soviet position was considerably more complex. On October 12, I met with the Soviet ambassador to inform him that we had shot down some Tupolevs of a type that the Iraqis had agreed to use only against Israel. I also told him that we knew they were secretly supplying arms to the Iraqis despite their promises to the contrary, that the barbed wire along our border had been removed, and that we had observed unusual troop concentrations in the Soviet Union.

I also brought up the problem of spare parts, which the Soviets had sold us without difficulty during the Shah's reign but which we had been unable to get for quite some time now. The ambassador gave me some vague explanations and promised to consult his government.

Later that same day, the Turkish ambassador brought me a message from Carter, who proposed forcing peace on Iraq if we would release the hostages. I responded affirmatively and forwarded Carter's message to Khomeini, which, as always with him, had the opposite effect from the one expected. He concluded that with Carter supporting us, we could continue the war.

The connection between the hostages and the continuation of the war became increasingly obvious. Every imaginable rumor was heard in the United States. Our representative there, Shams Ardekani, sent me a report describing Henry Kissinger's plan for Iranian Khuzestan. Apparently, he proposed solving the Arab-Israeli problem by separating Khuzestan from Iran and establishing it as a Palestinian state, which, because of its oil and gas reserves, would become the richest in the region. I also happened to know that Brzezinksi had assured Saddam Hussein that the United States would not oppose the separation of Khuzestan from Iran, despite the fact that Carter had promised to prevent our defeat. How could they give us such assurances while at the same time

•

agreeing to the dismantling of our country? I concluded that an ideological war must be raging in the United States as well. Carter may not have wanted to see Iran defeated, but other Americans very definitely did. For them, Iran was useless, except perhaps as a buffer against the Soviet Union, but Khuzestan could serve the same purpose and at the same time provide a solution to the Palestinian problem. I explained it to Khomeini this way: If the anti-Iranian faction wins, the area of Iran will be reduced to the Kavir Desert. Thus, Carter's assurances, as reported by the Swiss ambassador, were not to be taken at face value.

My political analysis was simple. The stage was being set for two changes, one in the United States and one in Iran. With Carter and Bani-Sadr out of the way, the field was open to Reagan, Beheshti, and Khomeini.

The Soviet ambassador paid me another visit on October 24, and this time he answered all my questions. He announced that his government was ready to deliver the 222 antiaircraft guns it was supposed to have delivered long ago. One last point. He denied outright the aid to the Iraqis, the Tupolev affair, and the threat on the border. The only positive note was his confirmation that they were pressuring Iraq to stop the war, the continuation of which, he claimed, benefited only the Americans. During this same visit, he presented me with a plan for guaranteeing the security of the Persian Gulf and asked me to have our government discuss it and give him an answer. My answer was instantaneous and negative. The security of the Gulf is the exclusive concern of the Gulf countries.

I received the French ambassador the same day. I wanted to urge his country to take steps to defend democracy in Iran by dissociating itself from American policy in the region. He answered that the hostages had become a political stumbling block for Europe, the absence of which would have enabled it to act independently of the Americans.

The diplomatic ballet continued. The Indian ambassador came to see me on October 26 to explain the two problems that, according to Saddam Hussein, prevented Iraq from concluding peace. The first concerned the export of our revolution, which supposedly threatened the stability of the other regimes in the region. The second had to do with our border, which, he claimed,

•

posed a constant threat to Iraq. Saddam Hussein was lying, for we had never massed troops on our borders to export our revolution. If exporting revolution means wanting to serve as a model to others through one's values, principles, and methods, how can you prevent it? Because of the war he started, our ideas were likely to spread faster than ever. When Europe declared war on revolutionary France, the ideas of 1789 spread much more rapidly than the despots of the time could ever have imagined.

We had to make the Iraqis understand that war only serves the existing dictatorship.

The Cuban foreign affairs minister, representing the non-aligned countries, arrived on October 28 with a message from Saddam Hussein, who accepted the return to the international border followed by a ceasefire and the abandonment of Iraqi sovereignty over the entire width of the Shatt-Al-Arab waterway. The Cuban minister proposed a five-point peace plan, explaining that he had not yet obtained Iraq's approval. This, of course, gave him a way out if I rejected it. This plan could be summed up in three lines: return to the border, ceasefire, acceptance of the 1975 Algiers Agreement, the organization of a nonaligned peace-keeping force, and negotiations to settle all the other problems.

I agreed, even though this plan did not satisfy all of our demands. The Supreme Defense Council officially approved the plan—it could not do otherwise—but made some corrections to prevent Iraq from renewing its aggression. The amended plan was sent off to Baghdad. The Cuban minister then returned to explain that to avoid any incident after the ceasefire, Iraq agreed to withdraw its forces several kilometers behind the border if we would do the same. The zone between the two armies would remain neutral until the conflict was fully resolved. For me, this was an important military victory as well as an especially significant political victory. The rest was up to the Iraqis.

On November 15, the Soviet ambassador informed me of the discussions that Soviet officials had had with Tarek Aziz, the Iraqi foreign affairs minister, during his visit to Moscow. According to the ambassador, the Soviets had managed to persuade Aziz that the war was not in the interest of any country in the region. The Soviet Union might be singing the praises of peace, but Saddam Hussein would never have attacked us had he not received strong assurances of success. I asked the ambassador, who had given Saddam these assurances, the Soviets or the Americans? Both, perhaps, because everyone knows that Iraq's military equipment is Russian and its political and financial support is American. Speaking more generally, I told the ambassador that the war in Afghanistan and the revolution in Iran demonstrated that the two superpowers were nearing the end of their expansionist phase and that henceforth all of their actions in the region would have repercussions, even in the Soviet Union. A traumatized Iran could become a problem for its Soviet neighbor, which would not be the case with a stable, developing Iran. I wanted to make the Soviets understand that it was not in their interest to assist the Americans in this war. The threat was thinly veiled when I reminded him that the Islamic part of the Soviet empire still had not accepted communism seventy years after the revolution and it rejected Soviet domination. Its inhabitants had lived with us for centuries, and if they were free, they would choose us. I wanted him to be aware that "total war" also meant war within empires.

Why should the superpowers feel free to stir up conflicts among us when we can return the favor by awakening the aspirations of the peoples they dominate?

When the Iraqis attacked us, we had only one objective: to prevent disaster. We knew that they had planned a two-week war; after that, they would have to ask their American and Soviet partners to resupply them.

We were in the same situation, but we had no outside assistance. Logistics was our biggest problem. We needed trucks, tank transporters, and communications equipment. As for the rest, the Pahlavi regime had, over the course of fifty years, bought enormous quantities of arms and ammunition—not all usable but sufficient for our war.

October 15, 1980, marked the end of the major Iraqi attacks. Our strategy then consisted of weakening the enemy with pinpoint strikes, then launching a large-scale offensive to try to end the war before Reagan took office. I wanted to use the peace as a strategy for strengthening democracy in Iran, inaugurating an independent international policy, and preventing the United States or the other major powers from dragging us into a lengthy war that would allow them to control the revolution.

•

THE COUNTEROFFENSIVE

In early November, Reagan was elected, but he could do nothing. Carter was defeated but still in office. We had only a short time to end the war, so I introduced the slogan "Every hour's delay could be fatal."

Aware of the danger, the mullahs stepped up their campaign to demoralize the army. We needed time to prepare for this attack in the best conditions possible; activity on the front was therefore cut to a minimum. The Beheshti-Rafsanjani gang and their thugs took advantage of the situation and the clergy's ignorance to say that the military was doing nothing since the front was quiet. One day, Ahmed Khomeini telephoned to invite me to his father's house, along with the chief of staff, Valliollah Fallahi, and the commanders of the three armed forces, Zahir Nejad, Fakouri, and Afsali. A very strange meeting indeed. When we arrived, we found ourselves in the presence of the sub-prefect of Abadan and several Revolutionary Guards.

We were immediately placed in the position of defendants on trial. Khomeini turned the meeting over to the young sub-prefect, who embarked on a virtual indictment of the army, which was nothing but an assortment of lies and approximations. The provocation was so obvious and so crude that we very easily turned the situation in our favor. The military officials then reproached Khomeini himself. "Your summoning us to answer to this young man is unthinkable. We have the armed forces, the fate of the country, in our hands. Such distrust is fatal to the future of Iran."

Khomeini realized that he had committed a serious blunder and, as always in such cases, tried to cover it up by reassuring and encouraging the officers. Immediately after leaving, I sent him a very firm letter denouncing these methods of demoralizing the army and asking Khomeini to spare my wife and children if, as rumor had it in Tehran, I was going to be assassinated.

In this same period, the mullahs contacted several military leaders to offer them the responsibility of conducting the war if I was relieved of my duties. The officers were quick to report this to me, adding that they refused to serve as tools in the clerics' quest for power. Typically, the mullahs simultaneously initiated

•

a campaign to demoralize the army while they offered important responsibilities to the officers.

In this environment, we prepared the plan that was supposed to enable us to impose peace on the Iraqis on our terms.

We first had to solve the logistics problem. All of our previous offensives had failed because we had no way of preserving our gains and protecting the divisions that always achieved results in the early hours of the attack. The soldiers immediately pointed out that the military manuals teach that the aggressor must be twice as strong as his opponent. We would never be twice as strong as the Iraqis and we could never match their resources. Should we give up, then? Our men were trained for classical combat; guerrilla techniques were inapplicable. Our only choice, then, was to create conditions that would allow us to attack, even from a position of inferiority.

We decided to use water to flood a large part of the land in the enemy's path. We envisioned a system of dykes that would allow us to open a corridor whenever we wanted it so that our divisions could pass through at a specific point. This way, we could neutralize part of the enemy forces. We solved the problem of helicopters flying over open terrain by coordinating the ground and air forces. The artillery covered the helicopters, making it possible for them to travel with a minimum of risk. This war produced so many innovations that General Fallahi, a professor at the War College, told a group of officers that he had learned more in a few days of combat than he had in thirty years of teaching. Outnumbering the enemy two-to-one and having an enormous, American-style logistical capability are not always possible. Military know-how had to be adapted to the circumstances.

The attitude of the Iranian officers was changing, and this is one of the reasons why we were able to resist so successfully.

We also knew that the Iraqi army was demoralized, that its penchant for sacrifice was diminishing, and that disputes between Shiites and Sunnis were beginning to erupt within the ranks.

To prepare for this offensive, I asked Ali Khamenei—who later was "Guide" but was then Khomeini's representative on the Supreme Defense Council—to come to the front. He was a member of the Islamic Republic Party, but I was convinced that

•

he was not involved in the agreement with the Americans. We took stock of the situation. I insisted on the fact that the relations between the military and the Islamic Republic Party were worse than the relations between the Iraqi army and the Iranian army. I asked him to call a truce between his party and the army. Then, to allay his fears concerning the risk of a takeover by me or the army following a military victory, I promised to resign as soon as the hostilities ended. He seemed to be convinced and I thought that he would act sensibly.

On the diplomatic front, I tried one last time to persuade the European ambassadors to intervene politically with the Iraqis to get them to withdraw their forces or, failing that, to give us the resources we needed to repulse them. They all mentioned the hostage problem as the stumbling block. This was only a pretext, however, because they knew about the agreement with the Americans. If the diplomats were to decide today to break the silence their position imposes on them, they would admit that the Reagan-Rafsanjani-Beheshti agreement was common knowledge in all of the diplomatic circles in Tehran.

Given this litany of refusals, we had to make do with what we had. First, we collected everything in working order and then we defined an objective. We decided to finish off the Iraqi divisions on the Ahvaz front, the effect of which would be to split the enemy forces down the middle. We tested our flooding system, which worked very well and which we were able to regulate according to circumstances. The same could not be said, however, of the idiotic plan suggested to Khomeini by the prefect of Khuzestan, Mohamad Gharazi, the current communications minister. His idea was to flood the entire region by blowing up dams. He and another cleric had convinced the Imam that it was the only way to save Ahvaz, which was on the point of falling. Mostafa Chamrah, an academic specializing in this sort of operation, came to warn me that this insane prefect was going to destroy an entire province—cities, villages, and whole cultures would be swept away—without any assurance that the Iraqi army would even be affected by it. Moreover, Khuzestan's hot climate would have dried the ground in two months, the Iraqis would have been able to resume their advance, and everything would have been destroyed for nothing. Fortunately, we were able to stop this absurd plan before it was too late.

We also needed to increase our manpower. We therefore released the officers and noncommissioned officers who were in prison. Khalkhali set 270 free in a single stroke. He appeared before the revolutionary tribunals shouting, "You want to keep them until the Iraqis come to set them free. Let them go. If they succeed, good; if not, at least they will die for something." I sent these officers to reorganize the Khuzestan divisions. I assigned one commander, an expert on helicopters discharged from the army because of his nationalist sentiments, to repair and adapt to the terrain the six hundred helicopters we had out of a total of eight hundred. He managed to turn them into a formidable weapon, even on the open plain.

There are two and a half hours of travel time between Desfoul and the Karkheh Kour front, where we had decided to attack. It took us over a month to transport all the equipment we needed. The inadequacy of our heavy transport equipment was responsible for this delay. We had transporters for tanks weighing from 30 to 40 tons, but our Chieftains weighed 70 tons. This is additional proof of the corruption in the Shah's regime. Another example: Soviet-made tank transporters could only carry Soviet tanks. We had a great many tank carriers but very few Soviet tanks. Even worse, they only worked on flat terrain. As soon as they started up the Khuzestan hills, the engines stalled.

This logistics problem distinguished us from the Iraqis throughout the war. They always had the means to move their equipment from one end of the front to the other in a matter of hours.

To create a diversion and immobilize part of the enemy troops, we launched a smaller offensive near Abadan at the same time as the Karkheh Kour operation. This attack, which occurred on January 2, 1981, was not given a name because I always refused to give sacred names to offensives, as the mullahs later decided to do. For me, war is horror, the work of Satan; therefore, it should not be sanctified. We achieved our objectives in a few hours. Our men's devotion to sacrifice was out of all proportion to that of the Iraqis. We immediately took nine hundred prisoners and then ran out of ammunition; otherwise, our momentum would have allowed us to complete the operation that day. Because we had to wait overnight for reinforcements, the Iraqis had time to group forces for a counterattack. At dawn on January 3 we were hit by seven consecutive waves, which halted our advance. I was alone in an armored vehicle, trying to get some rest, when an adjutant informed me of the Iraqi counterattack. I said to myself, "It's all over." Until midnight, I experienced some of the worst moments of my life. Our troops were running helter-skelter, trucks were retreating over the dry riverbed, and officers were running behind trying to stop them, but in vain.

The situation was deteriorating by the minute, and Ahvaz was going to be taken in a few hours. With the commanding general of the division, we raced up the line of trucks and stopped the first one. We were in complete disarray; the soldiers were shouting, desperate to escape at any cost. A colonel was weeping. In his half-Turkish, half-Persian accent, which I know well, he cried, "Do not abandon our country! Come back!" They saw me in the middle of the road, shouting, "Where are you going? Where are you going?" They all started crying, and then the officers regained control of the situation.

The trucks turned around and resumed their positions. We spent the entire evening looking for lost trucks. I stayed with some of them until eleven o'clock at night.

While all this was going on, about thirty officers, noncommissioned officers, and soldiers were around me when, in the middle of the night, "the organs of Stalin" (unguided rockets) began whistling. Suddenly, an officer quoted a verse from the Koran, threw himself on me, and knocked me to the ground. He was enormous and I could not breathe. A shell had just fallen between us and a gasoline truck. It landed two meters away from us in a bank of loose soil, without exploding. The soldiers crowded around me and began shouting exultantly. It was then that I understood the role of the irrational in war. This event totally changed the army's morale. The soldiers said, "God is on our side because of this miracle." The earlier, chaotic episode was forgotten.

Despite our efforts and the courage of the soldiers, we failed. We resumed our positions without gaining any ground. This failure in the field was offset somewhat by the extremely low number of casualties. The results of this operation were unremarkable. We should have ignored Khomeini's impatience and launched the attack two weeks later, as planned; then, our logistical problems would have persuaded us to choose a site more accessible from the rear. On the other hand, our speed of execution and our knowledge of the terrain turned out to be better than the enemy's. In a meeting of the Supreme Defense Council, one of the generals presented the long list of equipment we needed. I asked the mullahs a question: "Four months ago, when you wanted to solve the hostage problem, you promised us weapons. Where are they? Admit it, you won't get them until you get rid of me." I believe that all of these conversations were recorded. Maybe they will be heard someday.

In a message to Khomeini the day after this defeat, I asked him to publish the letter of resignation I had written to him the day I took office to assure him of my intentions. I mentioned all the pressure the clerics had exerted to speed up the offensive and their efforts to demoralize the army, Montazeri's in particular. It was the perfect time to get rid of me without any fuss, because I was proposing my own resignation. He did not accept it. Why? His refusal has always baffled me. Perhaps he was not fully supportive of the agreement concluded by the mullahs. There is still some doubt in my mind about this. One thing is certain, though: he feared the reaction of the army, which he still had to rely on since the Guards were not strong enough to bear the weight of the war alone. He knew that the Iraqis had every intention of continuing the war and were threatening Ahvaz. In addition to not answering my message, he gave a violent speech criticizing the mullahs and the Islamic Republic Party. Without mentioning him by name, he accused Montazeri of making irresponsible statements and preventing the president from doing his job. A few days later, he sent me a very encouraging telegram and forced Montazeri to publicly reaffirm his support for me. Apparently, the purpose of this gesture was to pacify the army, which felt betrayed by the government.

My position was not so bad, then, especially since among the country's social groups, the balance of forces tended to work in my favor.

10

THE ARMY AT THE EYE OF EVERY STORM

THE ARMY WAS RESPONSIBLE FOR FIGHTING THE WAR, THE army, spearhead of the old regime and victim of the revolution, we knew not at all—or only slightly—because, under the Shah, it was considered a secret society, governed by its own laws, with no connection to the civilian society it dominated. Even within the military institution itself, mystery and intimidation were the rule. No one was supposed to know what anyone else was doing. The man in the street considered the army a product of the superpowers. In Iran, an official study of the army was impossible. No researcher ever addressed the subject, not even its more accessible aspects such as recreation or sports. This mystery had its limits, however, since the Americans knew all that there was to know about our army, even things the Shah was unaware of. Proof of this was furnished in the final days of the regime when the American general, Dutch Huyser, was sent to take command of the armed forces. In these conditions, it was tempting to investigate the army, as the nationalist opponents of the regime did.

During the revolution, contradictions kept alive within the military institution for decades were brought to light. We then realized that about 90 percent of the army's power depended on this mystery.

The barracks were thrown open to the people, who wanted to know what this mysterious society, which had suddenly been stripped bare, was hiding. This forced exposure to civilian society did more to demoralize the army than to disorganize it. The uniform, formerly synonymous with power, became a symbol of weakness. We used to say that if General Razmara, the Shah's prime minister who was assassinated in 1950 in the doorway of a mosque, had gone there in uniform instead of civilian clothes, his assassin would never have dared to kill him. The Iranian people suddenly realized that the army was a social group like any other, with its faults, its weaknesses, its inconsistencies. The same thing is happening today with the Revolutionary Guards. The people are trying to find out who these bearded maktabis are.

The veneration of mystery is an ancient tradition in our society. In fact, the first modern professional army in Iran, the Cossack Brigade, was created by the Russians only about 110 years ago (1881). Prior to that time, the tribes that banded together to attain power and preserve it each had their own warriors. The mystery invariably surrounding these alliances has continued to the present day.

Secret investigations of the army, conducted during the Shah's reign, revealed five areas in which the country was critically dependent on foreign powers.

The first and most disastrous was logistics. The Shah himself said, "We can wage war for two weeks without importing equipment; our aim is to extend that period to four weeks and then to two months." When war arrived, our army's ability to resist exceeded the Shah's expectations, but logistics quickly prevented any significant gains, especially since an economic and military blockade made it impossible for us to get the arms and ammunition we needed.

The second area of dependence concerned the organization of the army, which was based not on the necessities of terrain, climate, neighboring countries, and other armies, but on a multinational model in which the Americans played the leading role. In the event of a third world war, all of these armies would function as pieces of a puzzle put together by the parent army of the United States. In terms of organization, weapons, and culture, our army was identical to the Israeli and American armies. Our air bases and our communications networks were wholly adapted to the exigencies of a war in which the Zagros Mountains would serve as a line of defense against the Soviet Union. The duty of our army was to hold out until its allies could react and enter the war. Thus, the organization of our military institution was based not on Iran's needs, but on those of a foreign power.

The third area of dependence was cultural. Each army generally reflects the culture of the country it serves. This was not the case with us, because our army's culture was foreign. In Iran, even an ordinary soldier was distinguished by his culture, which was different from the traditional national culture. Our problem was the integration of these two cultures. Could the young people who overthrew the Shah, who made fun of the "American way of life," fight a war in an army commanded by officers trained in another culture? This incongruity was felt even in daily life. Nourished by his American military culture, the officer lived in his quarters, far behind the lines, with his own room and a shower, and a mess to go to every evening to drink with his buddies. This type of life was shocking in an Islamic environment. That is precisely where the Israeli army differs from the Arab armies. The Israeli army exists within the culture of the Jewish people, whereas the Arab armies do not exist within the culture of the Arab peoples. This is one of the great weaknesses of the Iraqi army, for example. When we took prisoners, their belongings were brought to me—photos, magazines, anything that might explain their way of life. I quickly saw that the Iraqi army was more westernized than ours. The officers smoked, drank, carried pornographic magazines, played cards. I believed that an officer attached to all of these material things could not accept the idea of sacrificing his own life. I knew that in case of extreme danger, a sudden, swift attack, he would surrender. I have never mentioned this before because this psychological aspect of the war was extremely important to us.

The fourth area of dependence was the army's thoroughly American training and education. At first, the soldiers did not know how to use their equipment in the field because their American instructors had told them that a given weapon could

•

only be used in a given situation. The soldiers' training was perfectly adapted to the type of warfare employed by the American and Israeli armies, but no provision had been made for any other type of conflict. Our helicopters, for example, could be seen for miles on the Khuzestan plains; the same was true of our guns and tanks. In the first few weeks following the Iraqi attack, this form of dependence taught us something important: if we could adapt our equipment to the terrain, we could stop the enemy's advance. We failed, unfortunately, because our soldiers' lack of practice prevented us from making the most of the limited resources we had. There was something even worse. We quickly realized that gun manufacturers are not concerned about supplying equipment suited to the conditions of the buyer countries; all that matters to them is the sale.

Finally, the fifth—and by no means the least—area of dependence concerned financial resources. Our army depended entirely on oil revenues for literally everything, from the purchase of weapons to the salaries of foreign experts and the soldiers' pay. A saying we had summed up the situation perfectly: "More oil, more army." In our military tradition, however, the tribal armies were financially independent because of their plunder from their raids. The Iraqis were also dependent, but to a lesser degree because they could rely on the oil of the other Arab countries.

THE ARMY: TARGET OF THE MULLAHS

How could a war be fought with an army like this, an army no longer shrouded in mystery, an army afraid of its own shadow and of the future? Prime Minister Rajai seized every opportunity to tell everyone that if the war were won with this army, it would immediately cause problems for the regime. The army was the mullah's favorite target. They were actually more afraid of an Iranian military victory than they were of an Iraqi victory.

The officers often expressed the same thought: "What good is winning a victory if we are going to be its first victims? The mullahs are afraid of us and will slaughter us as soon as we lay down our weapons." The soldiers knew that they were in danger whether they won or lost.

Under the Shah, the army and power were one. Since the revolutionary victory, power, now separate, demands that the army wage war on its behalf; what was logical before no longer is. Certain soldiers went so far as to say: "You mullahs have the power, so you should fight the war." Apparently, the problem between the regime and its army still exists because there is now talk of dissolving the corps of Revolutionary Guards. The antagonism between the army and the regime is one of the reasons why the war lasted eight years. An army is not kept at war for so many years without good reason, such as the defense of the country, of power, or of democracy. The mullahs made power their number one priority and they made it clear that this was so. How, then, could they possibly convince the army that it was fighting for anything other than the perpetuation and consolidation of a religious dictatorship that the army rejected and that threatened its very existence? Although the army, despite heavy odds, fought a war which the mullahs used to consolidate their own power, it would pay the ultimate price: after I left, the army was gradually eliminated and replaced by the Revolutionary Guards.

During this period of the war, although the front was stabilized, the army was embroiled in conflicts within the regime. The Guards began a psychological war to discredit the army. They decried its so-called inertia. They went to Qom to goad Montazeri into provocation in the Friday prayers. He went even further and demanded an immediate offensive. In fact, the mullahs were urging the attack in hopes of a defeat, which would fit in with their plans and lead to my resignation. The Supreme Judicial Council and the revolutionary tribunals lent a hand by summoning officers on the slightest of pretexts and sending mullahs to the front to intimidate the soldiers. I issued an order to eject any mullahs entering military quarters without permission. I paid dearly for it because Khomeini later used this order against me. A tribunal could stop a requisitioned truck in the middle of the road on the pretext that its owner wanted it back. It was an excellent method of paralyzing the army.

At this time, the level of corruption in the old regime was revealed to us in all its enormity because, in theory, we lacked neither trucks nor aircraft. The desert was full of them. The mullahs went up in a helicopter and when they saw hundreds of trucks lined up, they exclaimed, "You have all that and you want to requisition other people's trucks as well?" In fact, most of the trucks were either in poor condition, unsuitable, or too old.

The Islamic Republic Party newspaper published articles every day denouncing both me and the army. The mullahs openly rejected the possibility of an army victory because it would make the army want to govern. They insisted that they did not want to compromise the revolution because of the war with Iraq; it would be better to sacrifice the army.

Reports piling up on Khomeini's desk announced, among other things, that I was organizing an army of 10,000 men to eliminate him and make myself the Bonaparte of Iran.

Another thing demoralizing the army was the legislation on the military service of the Basij, which the deputies, siding with the Revolutionary Guards, had passed in parliament. It called for the attachment of these young men to the Revolutionary Guards, whereas they were previously under the commander in chief of the armed forces. The law also gave the Guards priority in recruiting the Basij. The officers viewed this appropriation of human resources as a stage in the suppression of the army. Khomeini did not react.

A DEMOCRATIC ARMY

Turning these difficulties to advantage, I mobilized the army by explaining that its only chance of survival depended on a quick victory, before the Guards—who still numbered only 20,000—could become their rivals. I also wanted to take this opportunity to reorganize the army along democratic lines with a view to encouraging initiative and a sense of individual responsibility, from the top of the chain of command to the bottom. They clearly understood where their interest and their only chance of survival lay.

During this period, the relations with the Americans disturbed the army. Certain officers reasoned as follows: "Of course, we depended on the United States during the Shah's reign, but we were in control of the region then and if the Iraqis had attacked

•

us, we would have had the means to tear them to pieces. Now, there are two strategies, one giving us strength but making us dependent, and the other giving us independence but making us weak." This line of reasoning raised a question since we were suffering a drastic shortage of the weapons and logistical resources needed to launch serious attacks. Should we enter into secret relations with the Americans and the Israelis? The officers asking the question urged me to contact the Americans because, they said, "If you don't, the mullahs will, and they'll get the weapons they need to destroy us." On the one hand, I knew that the mullahs had signed an arms agreement with Reagan. Committed to my country's independence, I was in a very uncomfortable position. I resisted the temptation. I also knew that even if I did sign an agreement with the Americans, it would do the army no good since the mullahs could prevent the delivery of arms to the front. I knew, too, that the Americans, who had also concluded agreements with the Arab countries, would never provide us with enough equipment to assure total victory. At most, they would give us enough to maintain the status quo.

My first concern for the army—demoralized and under attack on all sides from the mullahs—was to replace fear with hope, to instill a sense of sacrifice in place of the tendency to become immobilized. Each man needed to develop his abilities and be recognized according to his own merits. It was essential that obedience, which is necessary, be reconciled with freedom, which fosters initiative. Order comes from following rules and an established plan that allows the subordinate to obey instinctively. But he must also be able to refuse orders that are unlawful or not within the scope of military duties. We therefore abolished the principle of blind obedience, which was habitual under the old regime.

I began by taking a look at the relationship between the head of state and the army. The head of state must renounce all despotic power over the army; this is the only way to prevent the military from becoming the backbone of a new dictatorship. The head of state can have direct relations with the army only in case of exceptional events, such as external aggression or a serious internal threat. All power must come from the people and only from the people. The head of state must never receive even a

•

shred of legitimacy from the army. On the other hand, the army must never perform any duties other than military duties. As the defender of national freedoms, the army can ask the people to participate in the war effort, but without dominating them. Internal security and the protection of civil liberties are the province of the people. The army's job is to focus on external affairs. We therefore eliminated everything in the organization of the army that gave it control over civilian society. An army reorganized in this manner would have a chance to become popular at home and respected abroad.

In a discussion of this reorganization during a strategy session, an officer said to me, "If an army loses its pride, it becomes purely mercenary." He was referring to the humiliations the mullahs were heaping on him, which he considered worse than the people's contempt of the army under the Shah. I replied, "How could you stand it back then when a low-ranking American officer gave your general an order? Even if the mullahs humiliate you, it's not as bad as being scorned by an American corporal. You say that your pride has been destroyed; the fact is that you never had any since your army was used by a foreign power to dominate this country. The people fought a revolution against you, the tool of a foreign power. Don't forget it."

From that point on, rank, decorations, and awards were given on the basis of criteria having nothing to do with loyalty to superiors, to men in the Shah's court, or even to an American corporal. Awards were given solely for acts of courage or devotion to duty. A new army was emerging.

Ever since the beginning of the revolution, discussion of the Revolutionary Guards had been lively. I was opposed to them and I said so. The country did not need two armies. While we were planning the counterattack, Khomeini, in a private meeting, threw out an idea as a sort of trial balloon. "What would you say if the Guards and the army were combined? These soldiers have no morals; we should put a Guard beside them so that men with morals can influence those who have none." I strongly objected to this proposal, which was like giving a healthy man a crutch.

We had two different approaches to the problem of the armed forces. The mullahs wanted to form their own army and I wanted to change the structure of the existing army. They

•

opposed this reorganization to the very end because they did not want democracy, they wanted power. The initial results greatly disturbed them. A competent, disciplined army—a democratic army functioning as a true university—was unacceptable.

JANUARY 1981

Despotism Takes Root

ON JANUARY 21, 1981, RONALD REAGAN MOVED INTO THE White House. In this same period, dictatorship was taking shape in Iran. It would take another six months, until my ouster in June 1981, for it to become entrenched in all the institutions of power. It was no longer a question of a revolution repulsing an aggressor, but rather of one dictatorship making war on another. With Reaganism established in the United States and Khomeiniism in Iran, I was gradually forced out. This period was marked by uncertainty, and many things could have changed during these six months. Unfortunately, after our attack failed, we no longer had any means of imposing an immediate peace on anyone.

Several factors worked together to prolong the hostilities. As far as the military was concerned, we were still unable to obtain arms and I knew that my presence prevented any American shipments. This was one of the reasons why I submitted my resignation. Khomeini refused. I had no choice, then, but to remain and to deal every day with a hostile government. I knew very well that the length of the war depended on the relations between the government and me. If I managed to replace it, anything was possible; if not, what chance was there against a government that insisted on prolonging the war as the only means of solving internal problems?

I sensed that the mullahs, to achieve total control, were capable of anything because they had abandoned all hope of popular esteem, opting instead for the principle on which all dictatorships are founded: lead and dominate the population— by force, if necessary. This could only be accomplished with outside help and, in our case, with the approval of the Americans and Soviets, whose interests would not be served by an end to the conflict.

The Americans were especially unforgiving because we had changed the nature of OPEC and made it a tool in the hands of the Third World. The Americans wanted to regain the initiative, to create a kind of reverse oil crisis, which they succeeded in doing a short time later. What we had achieved through oil proved that the methods of our revolution were exportable. Consequently, the Americans wanted to take control of our revolution, of our country. For all of these reasons, I became pessimistic and predicted that the war would continue.

Political warfare was raging in every sector of the regime: cultural, religious, ideological. The despotic faction was gaining ground in the revolutionary organizations or committees, but the breach between the people and the oligarchy, between the so-called revolutionary organizations and the popularly elected president, was widening. Strains were apparent in the army, which, having honorably defended the country in conditions of extreme penury, was only just beginning to evolve into a national force. Certain officers, contacted by Beheshti's entourage, had received assurances of survival in exchange for abandoning the president. The temptation was real, but I knew that they would not hesitate for long because they feared that, under pressure from the Guards, the promise would not be kept and they dreaded the alienation that a pact with the mullahs would entail. In the end, they rejected the offer and remained loyal to me.

The question of obedience then came under close examination within the Guards and the army. To whom was obedience due: the authorities or the people? Previously, and at least as far as appearances were concerned, a symbiosis had existed between the leaders and the people, the Guards themselves taking the role of defenders of the revolution without thought of domination.

Everything was changing. The mullahs—more and more detested—made the people wonder. Many of the Guards responded unequivocally, "Yes, the power of the clerics must be obeyed. The people must obey Behesthi, not vice versa." However, the Guards were more easily manipulated than the soldiers, who once obeyed the Shah—the symbol of power—but who saw no reason for obeying Khomeini. To correct this, I explained every day that the army is responsible to the nation, that power comes from the people, that an army that betrays the people serves strangers.

I also tried to explain these concepts to the Guards, for whom obeying any power other than that of the people should have signified a departure from the principles of the revolution. Although this subject was not well received by the Guards, it did have an effect on the soldiers, whose attitude continued to improve. The army, freed for the first time in a hundred and fifty years from dependence on a foreign power—first the Russians, then the British, and, finally, the Americans—was becoming a national army. We learned, for example, that a soldier taken prisoner by the Iraqis had refused a blood transfusion. He preferred death to carrying enemy blood in his veins! The change in the army became obvious during this period. It is important to remember that the army was still responsible for defending the country. The 20,000 Revolutionary Guards were not enough for the task; moreover, they were stationed primarily in the cities. The people said, "The true Revolutionary Guards are Bani-Sadr's men on the front." Unlike the army, which was becoming a vital, unified corps, the Revolutionary Guards remained totally bound to their social and cultural milieu. Each city had it own Guards with different ideologies and different decision-making structures. They were more effective locally than they were nationally. Even today, after eight years of war and all the reverses it has suffered, the army—or what remains of it—can act at the national level, but not the Guards. Moreover, the Guards cannot be mobilized rapidly because of the many different command units to which they are attached. Some of them, such as those in Khorasan, for

•

example, would refuse any mobilization order from Tehran, while others ignored the directives of such and such an official.

Militarily, we were in a period of status quo. The army refused to play the compromise game with the Americans, we had given up on the idea of receiving arms any time soon, the Iraqis could neither advance nor retreat, and our problems could only be solved politically.

In early January 1981, the Islamic Conference was held in Taif, which I was supposed to attend, especially since I had rejected the candidate the government had proposed for the post of foreign affairs minister.

Prime Minister Rajai went to see Khomeini and then came back saying that the Imam forbade Iran's participation in the conference. Iraq would be there, but we were going to throw away this golden opportunity to raise our voices as the victims of aggression, possibly to convince some of the participants of the justness of our cause, and to affirm our desire for peace. I asked Khomeini for an explanation. He claimed that he wanted to avoid creating discord between me and the others. What he really wanted was to prevent Bani-Sadr from becoming the nation's spokesman in the international arena. One evening, I saw Saddam Hussein on Iraqi television, giving a speech at this conference. What a pack of lies and contradictions! And there was no one there to challenge him.

THE SUPERPOWERS ON GUARD

I paid particular attention to the initial actions and statements of the new occupant of the White House. The amount of space I would have to maneuver in depended largely on his attitude. The first signs were not encouraging.

In early February, he told fifty or so guests that "Carter was mistaken when he said that the Soviets would intervene if we took action in Iran." Strange, isn't it? This gives the impression that he took action. We know of no action taken by Reagan at the beginning of his administration other than the agreement with the mullahs.

A few days later, on February 12, William H. Sullivan, former

U.S. ambassador to Iran, said in an interview in *Matin de Paris* that the man who could bring the mullahs and the army together to govern Iran was Beheshti. In a way, Sullivan was unveiling his own plan. The interview was reprinted in Iranian newspapers, but the passage concerning Beheshti, the man for this coalition, was omitted. The newspaper people reverted on this occasion to an old custom from the days of the Shah, which consisted of giving a completely distorted translation of a text. Later that week, the *Herald Tribune* published an article by an American historian discussing the Iranian revolution in terms of the world's great revolutionary periods, which the author divided into three phases: victory, anarchy, and despotism. This analysis was not incorrect, but it clearly indicated that I was doomed.

On February 12, in a speech on the anniversary of the revolution, I discussed these three periods at length. I said that certain revolutions, such as that of the Prophet or the American revolution, did not go through these three periods for three reasons: the existence of an elite that believed in freedom, society's general level of awareness, and the absence of foreign intervention. In the United States, the revolution was also a war for independence. There was no foreign intervention; consequently, there was never any room for despotism. In the French revolution, however, foreign intervention led to the establishment of a dictatorship. The same thing occurred in the Russian revolution. I insisted that taking the Americans hostage was a serious mistake because a provocation of this sort could only lead to the third period, that of despotism, which we were in fact entering.

The mullahs stepped up their attacks on my foreign policy. I had become a tool of European imperialism, a supporter of Mao Zedong's theory of a European, Japanese, and Third World alliance against the two superpowers. Once again, I had to clarify my position, for there was a huge difference between my philosophy and that of Mao.

I believed that by changing our relations with the superpowers we could help the progressive forces in Western Europe transform the political face of Europe in order to identify areas of mutual interest. Since we were witnessing the end of superpower expansionism, this would not be achieved through confrontation

•

with the Americans and the Soviets, as Mao had believed. The Afghan revolution marks the limits of Soviet imperialism and our own revolution was an attempt to do away with the American version. Both conflicts unfolded in one of the world's most strategic areas. The two superpowers have come together in such a way that they now have only two options: direct confrontation or joint solutions to problems. They chose the latter. The question is no longer one of carving out spheres of influence, but of working together to solve the world's problems. Moreover, our war with Iraq was a bonus for the two superpowers since, to a certain extent, it was detrimental to the interests of Europe and Japan, who rely on us for their energy. It is important to remember that although Europe and Japan produce more than the United States, the Americans control international finance. All this suggests the possibility of other relationships with the European countries. Prior to this period, I had already proposed replacing the dollar with a mix of currencies to pay for oil. This position was radically different from that of the mullahs, for whom "all blasphemers are the same," as it says in the Koran. Khomeini added, "Neither West nor East, all." What does this "all" mean? No relations at all, or relations with all the world? By refusing to choose as partners those who are incapable of dominating us—in this case, the Europeans—the mullahs turned implicitly toward the Americans.

The time for decisive political choices was fast approaching. Ahmed Khomeini became very active. He had introduced a new slogan: "To put an end to these internal conflicts, let's get rid of Bani-Sadr and Beheshti and organize a new party." Privately, he told my advisers, "I mention this third party to help the president. First, Beheshti's Islamic Republic Party and any of your supporters opposed to this change will be eliminated; then, a new party will be formed with you at the helm, supported by the people. You're safe in any case."

This ploy fooled no one. I vehemently attacked this plan. History shows that when one group maneuvers between two others, the most radical one wins. In a dialectic of ambiguity such as this, the group advocating force benefits most from the situation. Ahmed Khomeini criticized me for publicly mentioning the hostage agreement, even though my statements had been extremely vague. Obviously, I had embarrassed Khomeini.

The Imam began attacking me indirectly. The most vivid illustration of this was the proposal concerning a third party. The mullahs, meanwhile, intensified their dynamic of violence. They distributed literature defending war and force in human relations. In response, I wrote articles daily about totalitarianism, both ancient and modern, from the French Revolution to Stalinism, including Hitlerism, Titoism, and the religious intransigence of the Middle Ages. I was fairly successful in this regard since our newspapers were selling better than ever and the people did not participate in this cycle of violence.

The mullahs went further and initiated a campaign of repression against my supporters, whom they arrested on the slightest of pretexts. They began disrupting my meetings. They hit people who attended or threw stones at them, without ever being brought to justice for it. Anyone daring to shout "Long live Bani-Sadr!" during a speech by Rafsanjani was whipped and sentenced to a year in prison. They also started a photo blitz by sending men to my meetings to wave photos of Khomeini or Beheshti in the midst of the crowd. In retaliation, my supporters plastered walls with my portrait, preventing television from broadcasting shots of their rallies because Bani-Sadr's picture was everywhere. To put an end to this, the government prohibited the posting of any photos except Khomeini's.

Violence was increasingly visible in the cities and even in the villages. A climate of civil war was developing. A manhunt was organized against my supporters. Unfortunately, the first deaths and serious injuries were reported. A new stage had begun.

12

IRANIAN SOCIETY IN TORMENT

AFTER FIVE MONTHS OF WAR, MY ECONOMIC ADVISERS GAVE me a comprehensive report prepared in conjunction with our banking institutions. It listed in detail all the ills of our war-ravaged economy. Our gross national product had taken a nose dive as a result of reduced oil revenues. Unemployment was up sharply, especially in the productive western region where the war was being fought. Wartime expenditures were causing galloping inflation, despite minimal imports. Capital was being drained from the country. Fewer imports of capital goods and machine tools slowed production. Our foreign exchange reserves were disappearing fast because of the freeze on our funds abroad and the decrease in our oil revenues. The problem of agricultural production was becoming critical. Ever since the days of the Shah, reforms had proliferated. The decline in production was so bad that we had to import everything, even wheat. Problems were multiplying in industry as well. No one knew anymore who owned the factories and who was supposed to manage them. Was ours a capitalist or a socialist system? Our industry, which had long been reduced to assembling goods manufactured abroad, was anemic. We had no internal production to replace them. The services sector was totally stagnant; in Iran, its function consisted solely of distributing imported goods, collecting payments, and transferring them abroad. The construction sector was completely stalled. To gain the support of rich merchants, the government had to close its eyes to their illegal speculation. As always in time of war, wholesalers made a fortune. Some later claimed to have made more money from the war than they did during the entire forty years of the Shah's reign. Investment—when there was any—had become almost unprofitable. Private individuals and companies no longer had any legal protection in their work. Qualified managers were becoming scarce. The ones who were here during the Shah's reign had been expelled. This was not in itself a great loss since their job consisted mainly of seeking government subsidies. In Iran, companies were created solely to siphon money. Unfortunately, those who replaced them knew neither how to siphon nor how to manage.

Control of the Iranian economy was becoming increasingly fragmented. In each city, the mullahs exercised unlimited economic power. They sent the Guards to seize factories, land, machinery, goods.

During this period of extreme shortages, styles of consumption not seen since the days of the Shah reappeared. Those in power wanted to advertise their new status by acquiring rare— and often costly—goods. The moderation of the revolution's early days was forgotten. Money was being spent in ways completely incompatible with the situation.

It is often said in the West that the clerics are opposed to consumption; this is not true. I was opposed to consumption myself because a country cannot break free from underdevelopment if it lives beyond its means.

During the Shah's reign, the mullah symbolized man dependent on the community; he was distinguished by his modest appearance. Today, he is distinguished by outward signs of wealth. Every day, Khomeini fumed, "Stop spending so much! Exercise a little of your former restraint!" But there was little he could do because it was the only way they had of affirming and sustaining themselves: a beautiful house, a beautiful car, a beautiful wife. I left Iran penniless and I have no savings; all my belongings were confiscated by the mullahs. They used to have nothing; but like the nomenklatura in totalitarian countries, they quickly made themselves rich.

Finally, the paradox to end all paradoxes: We had a shortage of energy! We had oil, of course, but not the equipment to refine it.

The word *disaster* is too mild to describe our economy during this period. I wrote to Khomeini, and I sent the director of banking to explain to him the seriousness of the situation. He understood nothing. All he saw in the graphs I sent him were the beautiful shapes and colors of the curves! He told me that economics is a science for fools and that man is above such vagaries.

The mullahs were responsible for this cataclysm. When they drove out the managers and professionals, they effectively drained the country of its brainpower. Worse still was the fact that the Islamic Republic Party had raised generalized corruption to a level unheard of in the days of the Shah.

POLITICAL PARTIES: A NATIONAL VICE

The economy was not our only crisis. With the ushering in of Reaganism and its ties with Khomeiniism, the suppression of political parties began. One party was dissolved before the war began, the Muslim People's Party of religious leader Shariatmadari. I opposed this action on principle, although I had no sympathy for the party itself, which was a disparate union of elements from the old regime. Khomeini had suppressed this party, but he made no official moves against any of the others because the effect on the people had been disastrous. In Iran, there always were many parties; it is a national vice.

A sociological study conducted in Iran in the sixties revealed that 176 parties had been organized since 1905, the date of the constitutional revolution. This figure remained unchanged until the revolution. According to this study, our parties were tainted with five original sins, the first being their ideology, which was almost always imported from the West, often without regard for the situation in Iran or Islam. Since the leaders could not risk open opposition to these values, the views they expressed were ambiguous. This lack of clarity had its corollary in the lack of an agenda. General ideas were tossed back and forth, but no specific proposals were made. Women's rights were discussed, for example, but no one on the Right or the Left was able to take a clear stand on the subject.

The parties' fourth handicap was the lack of political ethics. Everyone knew that the Shah's government was amoral. For the Iranian people, the words *amoral* and *government* were synonymous. However, for a party to gain popular support, its leaders had to respect political ethics and the morals of society. If the Shah was unfaithful to his wife, it was normal since he was the Shah. But if a politician did the same thing, he was in serious trouble! In Iran, we have a saying that two things are fatal to a politician: a weakness for women and an itchy palm. In our society, women must be defended and respected as mothers; this noble principle has been a part of our tradition for centuries. And politicians, whose job it is to represent the people, must not be corrupt. Very few parties honored these principles.

Finally, from 1905 to the present, all of the parties were organized the same way: an active leadership and a passive membership whose only function was to approve party officials. The parties, often without an activist wing, were merely tools in the hands of their founders. They were all afflicted with these flaws to a greater or lesser extent, and the Islamic Republic Party most of all. Its program was one of the most ill-defined. No one knew what its varying ideology was or what kind of polymorphic Islam it advocated. I always refused to join. Only its objective was clear: the monopolization of power. Rafsanjani often mentioned the one-party system in Algeria as the perfect solution for Iran. He prepared the ground by attacking the other parties, which, it must be admitted, had no popular base: Bazargan's National Freedom Movement of Iran, Mossadegh's National Front, the Tudeh Party, the Democratic Front, and many others.

I renewed my efforts to defend the existence of these parties, every one of which had advised its members to vote against me in the presidential election. The fact that I won 76 percent of the vote proves their lack of influence in the country. Nevertheless, it was my duty to defend these parties in the name of democracy and freedom.

In February 1981, there was no winner and no loser in the internal conflicts. Khomeini, well aware of this, employed the usual tactic of despots: rule by dividing. He endorsed certain parties merely to annoy others, including the Islamic Republic Party. He favored attacks with diffuse repercussions, but was not bent on the disappearance of all the parties.

Within the Islamic Republic Party itself, division into factions and subfactions was the rule. The leaders applied the successful formula of all totalitarian parties. Create internal conflicts and then let them mature, gain strength, and erupt so that the strongest element wins. They were so successful at this that Khomeini, no longer able to control the internal strife, dissolved the party on June 2, 1987.

The social organization of the country was no better than it had been under the Shah. Delegations came to me every day complaining of the tactics of the Islamic Republic Party. Merchants, workers, and managers all asked me to free them from the councils set up by the mullahs. They had reorganized the Bazaar by creating a revolutionary tribunal with a mullah at its head to exercise tighter control. This was a throwback to the days of the Shah, when the Bazaar was financially, legally, and politically fettered by the regime. The merchants were afraid to move because some of their leaders had been executed.

Managers were being replaced more and more frequently with the Party's own men; whether they were competent was of little importance. What a regression!

The people were not indifferent to this spectacle. They showed their support for me by paying money into an account opened in the name of the presidency of the Republic to aid the victims of war. This too was a source of conflict since government agents punished merchants who gave money to the president but not those who did the same for Prime Minister Rajai, who opened an account to compete with me. Nevertheless, I received 240 million *tomans* in six months. It was astounding. Our newspaper's circulation rose to more than 300,000 copies a day, popular petitions piled up on Khomeini's desk, and protest strikes were organized.

•

THE REGIME'S POWER BASE

The mullahs weighed the importance of the various social groups, especially women, who became yet another subject of controversy within the regime. The mullahs began by recommending that women wear a veil, knowing full well that any objection on my part would place me in direct conflict with Khomeini. I believe that women are free to wear it or not, as they see fit. I based my response on the expanding role of women in society, asserting that the emancipation of the people was impossible without the emancipation of women. During the Shah's reign, my wife and I had conducted a study on the sociology of women in the history of Iran. We had wanted to publish it, but, as if by accident, the manuscript disappeared at the printer's. We had developed another interpretation of Islam as it pertains to women, which made the repressive and coercive behavior of the mullahs inadmissible. My views on the role of women were inimical to the mullahs' ambitions. In my articles, I often referred to the position of women in Muslim society and said to men, "If you treat women like subhumans, you become incapable of love. Love implies equality. If you do not want to deprive yourselves of this essential dimension of human life, you must change your attitude and regard women as equal, if not superior." I expanded this subject to include the family. "If you behave like a dictator at home, how can you expect your country to have a democratic system? The two things are incompatible."

The mullahs so little appreciated these remarks that they mentioned the problem to Khomeini. "Under the Shah, our sons became Marxists; now our wives are becoming Banisadrists! What can we do?" Many of the women in Khomeini's family supported my views. In all fairness, it must be admitted that Khomeini was much more enlightened in this regard than the others. He decided that women could become deputies or ministers. Moreover, in his last years, he approved one of my old proposals: if a woman spends her entire life working at home, the family income must be shared by both spouses. This is now the law in Iran. The very fact that Khomeini's daughter is a university graduate is a revolution in itself. Never before had this happened in the family of an ayatollah. Among political groups, women

•

were the most active and the least vulnerable. The mullahs did not yet dare to attack, imprison, and execute women as they would later do.

Students had an important place in Iranian society. Their role under the Shah and in the revolution was decisive. At this critical juncture, they could have prevented the establishment of despotism. Unfortunately, at the end of a long process, the universities closed their doors in the summer of 1980, two months before the start of the war. The mullahs had been preparing the ground for some time by talking of Marxist indoctrination and counterrevolutionary plots in the lecture halls, and, of course, by organizing provocations. Their supporters in the universities were so few in number—2 to 3 percent—that the idea of allying the students to their newfound power was inconceivable. There was only one solution: closing. A few months after I was elected, they had already considered closing the university, although nothing at the time justified such an action. I of course opposed this idea by saying that no one in the country or anywhere else would understand it, especially since the university had struggled against the Pahlavi regime for years. According to Khomeini, the schools were being used as bases for counterrevolutionary activities. Rajavi, the leader of the Mujahedeen, later gave me documents and recordings proving the existence of the plot among the leaders of the regime. In a meeting, Ahmed Khomeini, Rafsanjani, and Beheshti had drawn up the plan they later submitted to the Imam for approval. Ahmed Khomeini was supposed to obtain my assent, but of course I refused to endorse any action so contrary to all my principles.

A few weeks later, the secretary of the Revolutionary Council Dr. Sheybani telephoned me to say that the Council had decided to close the universities. As usual, the decision was made while I was away. On returning to Tehran, I met with the Council at Rafsanjani's house to protest this action and to offer my resignation, the reason for which I intended to explain publicly. With the second round of legislative elections still ahead, they were panic-stricken. They shifted the responsibility to Khomeini, citing the armed terrorist activities allegedly being planned in the universities. To resolve this problem, I suggested ordering the closing of all branches of the political parties in the university, which should itself continue as an institution devoted exclusively to education. Seeing no other way out, they agreed, and so did Khomeini. I thought I had averted the danger.

The final exams took place as usual. The revision of the curriculum—"the cultural revolution," as they called it—was to take place during the summer to prepare for the return to a new university, one more oriented toward Islam. In the middle of the summer break, as the Rajai government was forming and war was brewing, Khomeini issued a statement announcing that the universities would remain closed until the cultural revolution was completed. I responded with a very harsh letter, accusing him of having set a new record in the suppression of freedoms. My concern was increased by the fact that the initial contacts had just been made with the Americans. In a U.S. embassy document I later obtained, the closing of the universities was listed as one of the ways of controlling the Iranian revolution. I did not have access to this document at the time, but Khomeini and the mullahs knew about it. According to the clerics, the university—opposed to Islam and the struggle against the generalized aggression of the Great Satan—was to be replaced by the Basij training centers they were pleased to call a university. The Islamic Republic Party, the revolutionary organizations, the committees, the tribunals, and even the Evin prison became universities that were to liberate the young from classic, anti-Islamic, imperialistic studies. Because they wanted me out of the way, far-Left parties such as the Fedayeen-e-Khalq also joined this campaign.

The doors of the laboratories, the lecture halls, and the classrooms remained closed. The mullahs deliberately smashed the crucible in which the vital, creative forces—the forces ensuring the renewal and the future of society—were forged. The philosophy of "how to live" was replaced by the ayatollahs' philosophy of death.

The merchants attracted everyone's attention. They considered themselves the initiators of the revolution since, by shutting down their businesses, they had caused the first demonstrations. Back in 1906 they had launched the constitutional revolution and, later, the movement for the nationalization of the oil industry. They were a force to be reckoned with. In early 1981, they were caught in a dilemma: on the one hand were the mullahs, who were very influential in the Bazaar, and on the other, the president and a large segment of the population. Whom should they trust?

The largest merchants quickly decided to join forces with Beheshti, rightly sensing that the largest profits were to be made on that side. The medium and small merchants were attracted to my theories concerning the nationalization of foreign trade. This measure is still an issue between the Left and the Right since Khomeini has decided to privatize foreign trade. In my opinion, nationalization was not an ideological measure. We were living in a foreign-dominated economy; we had only one source of income: oil. This national resource belongs to all. Why should a few individuals be allowed to appropriate it? I said that we had to budget oil revenues in order that our country might have an independent, constantly growing economy.

The mullahs' view was extremely simple: Oil is a profit to be divided up. Each group must get its piece of the cake, according to its influence. The medium-sized merchants were solidly behind me in this regard. This economically healthful measure allowed them to participate directly in the activities of importing, exporting, investment, and so on. Moreover, the new banking system we had established offered medium-sized merchants a means of escape from the domination of the large merchants, who were previously the only ones able to obtain credit from the banks, which they distributed as they saw fit. This support was extremely valuable to me.

The most bitter fight was with the working class. Opposing us were workers with Marxist and pro-Soviet leanings who were very active. The fact that they had never been able to play a decisive role either during or after the revolution made them even more so. Every Marxist-inspired coup attempt had failed. For them, the ideological debate concerned the concept of freedom, which some viewed as part of a bourgeois philosophy, but which others saw as a necessity for the working classes. Naturally, they advocated the establishment of democracy by a proletarian dictatorship. The second point at issue concerned the status of our revolution. Were we in the situation that enabled Lenin to fight the second revolution, or were we in the first stage of an internal, anti-imperialistic struggle taking precedence over our

•

primary struggle against outside imperialism? Their answer: We are in the Kerensky stage and must give priority to the internal struggle.

It was very hard for me to get through to them. A few Marxists—a very small minority at the time—broke away from this line of reasoning and advocated freedom. I repeatedly told the workers that it is the working class that needs freedom most. Dictatorships do not prevent the middle class from making fortunes. As for the establishment of a proletarian dictatorship in Iran, it was wishful thinking. There are only 400,000 workers, and not all of them can be defined as workers according to Marxist terminology. Ours is not an industrial society, we are not in Soviet Russia, and we are economically dominated.

With freedom, however, we could prevent the resurgence of a foreign-dependent middle class. I told the workers, "You must understand that if a dictatorship is established, you will produce wealth that others will take—not only the mullahs but foreign powers as well."

Most of the clerics opposed dictatorship. Many leaders encouraged me openly; others sent their aides to assure me of their support. Paradoxically, the students of theology were very afraid of Khomeini and vice versa. They supported me against the leadership of the Islamic Republic Party.

Khomeini did not like the students' viewpoints. In a speech, he angrily retorted, "I know that plots are being organized in the seminaries and in religious centers such as Mashhad. I will put them down, make no mistake." Montazeri, leader of the Friday prayers, answered him by telegram: "Don't worry, there is no plot. We are keeping a close watch." He then summoned all the Imams in Iran to Qom to organize an offensive against rebellious religious groups.

Since I played a determining role in this open warfare against the clerics' dictatorial tendencies, I decided to go to Qom to see how I would be received. I was surprised by the welcome, the devotion, the enthusiasm of the people—clerics included. This trip had a profound effect on Khomeini, who felt defeated on his own ground and therefore decided to speed things up.

The peasants' influence was minor, but I had many supporters among them. I had instituted a policy of agricultural development

•

and higher incomes, which pleased them. Moreover, in the villages, religion was viewed more as the cement holding society together than a restrictive individual practice.

If, at this point in our history, some sort of balance sheet had been prepared indicating the amount of support I enjoyed among the various social groups, it would have been seen that I was still in the game.

Aware of this, the mullahs embarked on a campaign to denigrate the people. They dragged out the old religious doctrines of the Christian Middle Ages to show that the people are ignorant. The purpose of this new tactic was to separate me from the people. I understood it completely; they would be able to say that Bani-Sadr was eliminated for deceiving an ignorant populace. They tried to distort the Koran, to make it say that the people know nothing, whereas its principle of Oneness teaches just the opposite. The Koran says that the voice of a community is God's voice, its hand is God's hand, and its conscience is nearest the truth. By insulting the people and discrediting them, the mullahs hoped to justify their disregard for the popular will.

The mullahs ventured into new territory when they announced that nationalism and Islam were incompatible. The decision to give Islam absolute priority had dire consequences for the country. Anything even remotely associated with the West was banned, with the notable exception of consumer goods. We were to hear no more of development, technology, experts, studies, scientific research. Again and again they said, "Guns are more important than progress because the time has come to defend Islam, to make war on the blasphemers of the world." The purpose of attacking nationalism as a Western concept was to place their religious power above all social values.

At the close of this period, the balance of forces was as follows. Kalashnikovs and assault weapons in hand, the revolutionary organizations held the cities. On the other hand, our views were gaining ground among the people. The mullahs found it extremely difficult to separate the people from their president. This difficulty alone delayed my departure, which the mullahs had planned to coincide with Reagan's inauguration. After all, $5 billion worth of weapons were at stake!

Since we cannot get rid of Bani-Sadr with the people's

•

support, we will go against the people and force him out. This line of reasoning explains the events of the four months remaining to me in Iran.

13

TOWARD CONFRONTATION WITH KHOMEINI

WE WERE IN THE SIXTH MONTH OF THE WAR. WITHOUT MY knowledge, the first arms purchase contracts were signed with the Israelis on behalf of the Americans.

Activity on the front was subdued. Within the country, however, we were facing a mountain of physical and ideological problems common to every revolution in the world. We counted twenty-one problems, ranging from independence to Islam and including the export of our principles, freedom, order, the role of organizations, poverty, inflation, and so on. Surveys revealed that as far as the people were concerned, these twenty-one problems boiled down to four: freedom, economics, security, and war. Toward the end of this period, in April, all of these problems dwindled to insignificance next to one major problem: leadership. Who should have power and how should it be used? The ideological battle during this period revolved around three major subjects: order or disorder, freedom, and Islam.

The mullahs, who are fond of proverbs, love to say that for them, "Order is disorder." Catholic priests know that they will receive a certain sum of money from the diocese each month and that their material wants are satisfied, at least minimally. The mullahs, however, did not receive money on a regular basis because the income from religious properties, collected by the state, was not always reimbursed to them. Thus, they lived from day to day on what they were given, without any provision or plan for the future. This way of life affected every aspect of the mullahs' political, religious, and cultural existence. According to these principles, they would normally have rejected despotism. But they did not reject it; instead, they wanted to apply the concept of disorder to the war. They imagined that the Iranian revolution had emerged from disorder.

In these circumstances, defending order was risky. I saw an enormous trap opening before me. In the minds of the people, the word "order" called up memories of the Shah's regime.

The mullahs devised slogans about disorder, their purpose being to place me in an impossible situation. I therefore broached this subject very carefully, especially since in leftist circles, the words "order" and "dictatorship" are generally associated. But did this mean that anarchy, followed by clerical totalitarianism, was inevitable?

I saw that I would have to give a new definition of order. I recalled that order can indeed be based on force, as it was under the Shah, but that it can also be the natural result of freedom and the spontaneous organization of the labor and social life of the country. In a society organized without the use of force, the concept of order is not dangerous. The people understood this quite clearly, the defeat at Khorramshahr having served as a vivid example of the consequences of disorderly warfare. I said again and again that the seventeen different groups defending the city had precipitated the disaster.

The people upbraided the mullahs in meetings: "You have lived in disorder for fourteen centuries and have prevented the Muslim world from moving, from advancing. Let Bani-Sadr put things in order and you'll be able to move beyond your traditional resistance to change."

Several deputies came to warn me that my stance on freedom and independence was in danger of being overshadowed by that of my rivals, who had found a new burning issue: the oppressed. I therefore adjusted my program to include changes in the social structure and an even more virulent attack against the

•

minority who were exploiting the revolution and the war. I explained the intrinsic relationship between freedom, independence, and social change as a means of eliminating inequality and injustice.

The effect of all these very simple explanations was to turn the mullahs' own rhetoric against them. They dropped these polemical subjects and settled on just one—Islam—which they ranked ahead of all other problems! In April 1981, Khomeini began saying that it was quite possible to disobey the law without thereby committing a sin against Islam. The aim of this statement was to make everyone understand that the law owed its legitimacy to him. It was as though General de Gaulle had said one day, "I drafted the constitutional law of the Fifth Republic; thus, it is I who give it legitimacy and I can apply it as I see fit."

Clearly, Khomeini was telling the people that Islam is above the law. This opened the door to every form of excess. It became dangerous to say that Islam was not the most important priority. The humanistic, progressive, tolerant Islam that I advocated was now at the opposite pole from his. I embarrassed the mullahs by asking them to explain the substance of the Islam they practiced. If not a path to freedom, independence, and progress, what is it? They had nothing to say because they had emptied Islam of substance. It was now embodied only by the Guide, who alone decided what was Islamic and what was not, despite his frequent 180-degree turns. A strange Islam was emerging, not unlike the Christianity of the Middle Ages, manifested in the infallibility of the pope. We were passing through the last phase separating us from religious totalitarianism.

The standard rhetoric of all fascist regimes began to be heard. It was said more and more frequently within the government that we must not endanger the regime by discussing its faults; the revolutionary organizations were sacred and inviolate. As in the Stalinist era, everyone had to keep silent to avoid imperiling the system and be willing to die, if necessary, for the sake of the regime. To cast doubt on the Guide was to side with the counterrevolutionaries.

To avoid falling into this fatal trap, we decided to criticize the system as often as possible. We chose to demystify the revolutionary organizations by pointing out their faults, and when they went too far, by denouncing them unsparingly. The fact that the revolutionary organizations never won popular support proves how effective our methods were. The mullahs and their whole set were so thoroughly desacralized that Islam was the only angle of attack they had left. They no longer ventured into other areas for fear of being outmaneuvered.

I experienced these conflicts not only as an elected official but also as a sociologist conducting an experiment on an entire society subjected to a series of painful and complicated trials: the war, the hostage affair, the intervention of the superpowers and that of the rest of the world, which directly or indirectly played a role.

During these two months, no matter what problem we addressed, I always ran into the same obstacle: the Guide—Khomeini—wanted to impose government by the mullahs at all costs. He even revealed the depth of his feelings on this subject to a cleric friend of his, Lahouti, who had come to ask him to do something about the troika of Behehsthi, Rafsanjani, and Khameini. Khomeini's response was, "I'll do whatever needs to be done with these three men, but one thing is certain: if we have to execute 50,000 people to establish the mullahs' regime, we will do it."

A POPULARITY TEST

On March 5, 1981, the day set aside to commemorate the death of Mossadegh, I planned to attend a memorial service at Tehran University. The Behesthi-Rafsanjani team had declared this day decisive. They wanted to test my popularity. A large turnout would be a plebiscite for me. They therefore called on militants in the revolutionary organizations to disrupt the meeting. At 2:00 P.M., a full report on these preparations was sent to me. I informed the interior minister of what was coming and asked him to stop the agitators. Moreover, Khomeini, who hated Mossadegh, warned me about what I was going to say. He did not look kindly on the president of the Republic—elected by popular vote— laying a wreath on the tomb of a man who symbolized democracy and independence in Iran. At 3:00 P.M. on the university campus, as I was about to speak, some people standing behind the gates started shouting "Bani-Sadr, Pinochet! Iran will not become another Chile!" They continued shouting throughout my speech and then threw stones at the crowd. The interior minister had done nothing, of course. I asked the crowd to eject them, peacefully. I wanted to prevail through the people, not through force, but I realize now that the necessary support was lacking. At the time, however, I thought it might be possible because the people crowding the campus and the neighboring streets were solidly behind me. Several of the agitators who were arrested carried cards attesting their membership in revolutionary committees. I filed a complaint against them, to no avail. Nevertheless, to remind the judiciary of its responsibilities, I asked the people who had attended the memorial service to go testify before the courts. The judges, frightened by the number of witnesses who showed up, asked me to drop the charges.

This date marks the beginning of the antagonism between the revolutionary organizations and the people. From this point on, the mullahs were forced to choose between the people and the organizations. Khomeini and the clerics were isolated and vulnerable. Two surveys conducted and paid for by my office and the Interior Ministry increased their discomfort. Only 6.5 percent of the people interviewed said that the president was wrong in his handling of events at the memorial service, while 90 percent said he was right. The newspapers published these findings, accompanied by a story about a group that had been assigned to assassinate me during the ceremony. One of the alleged perpetrators confessed, but once more, the judiciary did nothing.

To press my advantage, I again demanded a face-to-face meeting with the mullahs. Khomeini invited us to his home on March 15 to inform us that we were all henceforth forbidden to speak in public. Nevertheless, prior to this meeting, he had agreed to respect free speech, provided that I issue a statement repudiating all political groups opposed to the regime and that I say nothing about the agreement with the United States or the hostage affair. I agreed, despite everything, because I knew that open discussion—even about other problems—could lead us out of the ghetto.

Two events occurred during this period, revealing both the Imam's anxiety and the mullahs' determination. Khomeini's grandson Hussein came to see me, in tears. The survey, he said, frightened his grandfather, who, it seems, began to tremble while reading an editorial I had written saying that the people would soon become aware of the betrayals and crimes of the religious leaders.

Bazargan and his friend Sahabi, founder of the Iran Freedom Movement, warned me that, according to one of their sources, my rivals had decided to eliminate me, come what may, in order to expedite the agreement with the Americans.

When I traveled to Mashhad on March 20, the people turned out to cheer me, despite pressure from the local authorities, the prefect, and the governor, members of the Islamic Republic Party. Every day, I noted signs of encouragement from all levels of society. My popularity was growing. This was both an asset and a liability. I knew that in all societies there are two kinds of popular figures: those who, for one reason or another, enjoy a state of grace and then become unpopular as soon as the circumstances change, and those whose popularity increases with time because they know how to work across class and group boundaries, keeping the general welfare of the people constantly in view. The larger the field of action, the more popularity increases with time. If the field shrinks, popularity wanes.

I wrote these thoughts to Khomeini to make him understand that he would lose what popularity he had left if he forced the mullahs on the people. I quoted a verse from the Koran: "Only the guide who acts in the general interest of man is worthy of the grace of God." My point was that a liberator who symbolizes a specific category of men and then a political faction can easily become an oppressor.

At the close of this period, in the month of May, all of the elements necessary for a final confrontation between Khomeini and me were in place.

14

MAY 1981

Peace in Sight

IN MARCH, OLAF PALME CAME TO SEE ME. WE WERE ON VERY
friendly terms and could speak freely with one another. In a
private conversation, he told me that he was aware of an
agreement between the mullahs and the Americans, but did not
know exactly what it concerned. He knew, however, that I was
in serious danger. I asked for his help. I wanted him to use his
influence as a European friend of the Third World to defend the
democratic experiment I was trying to preserve in Iran. He
offered me his services and we agreed on a two-part mission.
First, he would go see Saddam Hussein to persuade him to end
the war, the continuation of which only benefited the Americans;
second, he would tour the European capitals to make the heads
of state understand that neither the Soviets nor the Americans
wanted Bani-Sadr. The Soviets feared a prosperous, democratic
Iran on their border, and the Americans, by choosing to support
the mullahs, rejected the establishment of a democracy in the
Arab world, especially in an oil-producing country of primary
importance to the world economy. He would also gently remind
his European friends that Iranian oil is consumed not by the
Americans but by them and the Japanese. I had complete

confidence in him. He was an excellent emissary who had proved himself on many occasions, especially with Chancellor Bruno Kreisky of Austria and Prime Minister Felipe González Marquez of Spain during the hostage affair. Olaf Palme's connections with his international socialist colleagues were an added benefit.

Immediately after Palme's departure, the Islamic Republic Party newspapers accused me of making a deal with Saddam Hussein through the former Swedish prime minister. They resurrected an old Tudeh Party slogan, claiming that I wanted to replace American imperialism with European imperialism. The Soviets were extremely sensitive to this issue, although in my writings I quite often criticized the Europeans, who, in my opinion, were unaware of the length and importance of the economic, cultural, and political crisis they were experiencing.

On March 1, eight heads of state representing the Islamic Conference—including Sekou Toure of Guinea, Zia ul-Rahman of Bangladesh, Zia ul-Haq of Pakistan, and Yasser Arafat—came to Iran accompanied by Habib Shatti, secretary of the organization. Sekou Toure, who must have thought that Islam was all that mattered to us, launched into a discussion of religion, despite the fact that we were there to negotiate. Then he broached the subject indirectly by saying that when a house is on fire, the fire must be put out first, before trying to find out who started it; the same is true of the war.

I responded, "I am pleased that you have come to ask me to end the war because it is contrary to everything our revolution stands for. But instead of coming here, you should have gone to Baghdad! We have been fighting for six months, despite the fact that Saddam Hussein was supposed to have crushed us in six days. Holding our own against a well-equipped army has been a real feat for us."

In a private meeting, I told them about sending Olaf Palme to ask Saddam Hussein to withdraw his forces so that we could conclude peace. The Soviet ambassador came to see me several times during this period. One important message he brought with him was his country's response to my repeated requests to buy arms. It was still no, of course, even regarding contracts signed and paid for during the reign of the Shah.

I was also very concerned about the Afghan problem. I sent

•

Yasser Arafat on a mission to the Soviets. I proposed the creation of a fact-finding mission to determine to what extent American forces were involved in the war in Afghanistan. If the Americans were not involved, the Soviets should leave the country. If the study showed that Americans were present, we would demand that they both leave. Arafat, at the very outset of his mission, informed me of the Soviets' displeasure. They considered the need for an intermediary between them and us highly irregular.

I had chosen Yasser Arafat for two reasons: he was an Arab, and it was good to have him representing us at a time when Saddam Hussein was describing the conflict as a war between Persians and Arabs. Moreover, this mission strengthened his international political stature. Arafat had already played an effective role during the hostage affair, while I was foreign affairs minister. The Iranian newspapers at the time had accused him of being an agent of the "Great Satan," which was untrue; he genuinely wanted our revolution to succeed and he knew that the hostages were our greatest handicap. I suggested to Khomeini that the women and blacks among the hostages be released to demonstrate our sympathy for the black minority in the United States and to refute propaganda claiming that we oppress women in our country. The Imam thought the idea excellent and agreed. We released thirteen hostages, with Arafat acting as intermediary. On another occasion, before the war, I had asked Arafat to persuade Saddam Hussein not to attack us. This third mission of Arafat's was short-lived because the Soviet ambassador, Vinogradov, came to see me to propose a discussion of the Afghan problem, which, for his government, concerned the neighboring countries as well, that is, Pakistan and Iran. No discussion was possible as far as I was concerned because the Soviet presence in Afghanistan was unacceptable. We share a common culture with the Afghans and the occupation is a threat to us, wedged as we are between Iraq on the west, the Soviet Union on the north, and Afghanistan on the east. I told my Soviet visitors over and over that the withdrawal of their troops from Afghanistan was an essential condition for any improvement in our relations.

In this, the sixth month of the conflict, certain objectives defined by the Americans were being achieved. The principle of

•

"no winners, no losers" in the war to gain control of the Iranian revolution was becoming a reality in the field, control over OPEC was being reestablished, and American contacts with factions within the regime were on the rise. Three other objectives described in the reports seized in the embassy were as yet unattained: using the Iran-Iraq war to gain a foothold in the Persian Gulf, stabilizing the regimes in the region, and establishing military bases for the American strike forces.

At the time, some of the mullahs in power were deliberately exaggerating the Soviet threat in order to deflect attention from the agreement, create ambiguities, and pursue their own agenda without attracting public notice. I tried to put things in perspective by saying that, yes, the Soviets did want to dominate us, but exaggerating the Russian threat would only obscure the real danger, which was control by the United States.

SADDAM HUSSEIN LOOKS FOR A WAY OUT

On March 29 and 30, 1981, the heads of state of the Islamic Conference, led by Sekou Toure, came to Iran for the second time. Immediately upon arriving, Sekou Toure and Zia ul-Haq requested a private meeting. I recall Sekou Toure's remarks quite clearly. "I am familiar with your difficulties, your problems; don't be afraid! I was on the losing side myself for ten years and I had to wait patiently before coming out on top."

I answered, "There is a great difference. I am a representative elected by the people and our experiences are completely different because in your country you have installed a dictatorship, which is a failure. Third World development through dictatorial regimes, whether Left or Right, will always be doomed to failure."

I was quite familiar with the regime of Sekou Toure and since I was not in the habit of hiding the truth, I explained to him that I did not want to duplicate his experience, but to establish a true democracy.

I had no intention of being a loser for ten years just so I could become a dictator someday, especially when I could become one right away if I would play Khomeini's game. Indeed, that was all

•

he was waiting for. He had given me full authority in the beginning, imagining that I would be a puppet in his hands, but I refused. What mattered most to me now, though, was Saddam Hussein's response to my proposals. According to Sekou Toure, he was ready to accept peace if we would make some gesture that would allow him to save face.

Specifically, the Iraqis offered to withdraw their forces if we would agree to conclude a new treaty to replace the Algiers Agreement of 1975, even if the terms remained virtually the same. Obviously, the purpose of this was to allow Saddam Hussein to pull out in the best possible conditions. It was unacceptable. When the 1975 agreement was signed, both regimes were unstable and both wanted to consolidate their position and resolve the problem in Kurdistan. It was for this reason alone that they agreed to locate the border in the middle of the Shatt-al-Arab waterway. In the interest of avoiding a resurgence of anti-Arab feeling, we had never questioned this agreement.

I was very frank with these messengers. I explained to them that I had very little time and that if we managed to conclude peace very quickly, it might be possible to save our experiment in Iran. There would then be no need for the secret agreement with the United States and the mullahs would no longer be able to resist a president, a commander in chief, who had thwarted an act of aggression. As I was leaving them I said, "Make Saddam Hussein understand that this month is the last chance; afterward, there will be no hope for peace! And I don't even know if I can hold out until you return."

I explained my position in the open meeting: refusal to reconsider the Algiers Agreement, simultaneous withdrawal of forces, a fact-finding commission to determine who started the war. To a certain extent, the envoys acted as the Iraqis' advocates in this meeting. I attacked Saddam Hussein, who was now rejecting the 1975 agreement because he wanted to create the illusion of strength. Did this mean that the basic principle is not law, but force; that we should fortify ourselves in order to annihilate the enemy? What we were seeking was peace based on law. From a historical perspective, we could have gone even further and claimed back several regions from Iraq, but we would not give in to chauvinism.

•

The Algiers Agreement was not in Iran's interest. A large portion of our territory was abandoned to the Iraqis by the Shah. Still, we did not question the agreement. The choice was Saddam Hussein's: history, which would be dangerous for him, or the agreement.

Everyone present agreed with me. Habib Shatti assured me that he would be Iran's advocate in Baghdad.

As for the war itself, we had consolidated our positions. Our irrigation system to control the front worked wonders; we were actually using it as a weapon. Moreover, we planned to retain this system and use it after the war to irrigate previously uncultivated land.

We were, however, running out of ammunition. The reserves we had in May would allow us to hold out for a month, but our plan for pushing the Iraqis back to the border required another four months of combat. Consequently, we had to achieve the impossible by switching our tactic to sudden, pinpoint attacks based on the element of surprise. Speed became our biggest asset. The heavy Iraqi war machine jammed frequently, and paradoxically, the enemy's superiority in arms actually became an obstacle to it.

Our efforts paid off. Between April 25 and May 1 we recovered half our territory.

Saddam Hussein wanted peace for other reasons. Public opinion in Iraq was more favorable to us than it had been at the beginning of the war because we persistently refused to respond in-kind to the bombing of our cities and because we treated prisoners of war very well. The Iraqi public also noted that after twelve years of preparation, its army—touted in official propaganda as the best in the Middle East—was brought to a standstill. Our contacts with dissident Iraqi intellectuals were very useful. I also knew that Saddam Hussein was worried about his political future. I had received reports of discussions between him and the Americans, who he criticized for not giving him more aid in the early weeks of the conflict. Since the Soviets were no longer supplying him with arms, the only suppliers were in Europe— France in particular. Olaf Palme's role was crucial during this period. If he prevented the Europeans from supplying arms to the Iraqis, we could decide the issue in the field. Saddam Hussein was mortally afraid of this possibility. He felt increasingly isolated from the rest of the region. Opposition between Syrian and Iraqi Baathists was on the rise. Moreover, the Iraqis did not look kindly on our friendship with the Palestinians. They were afraid of being caught between our two revolutions, although they are very different in nature. Nevertheless, these two popular movements could inflame the entire region. This is one reason why I assigned so much importance to Yasser Arafat in the negotiations, the Iraqis having specifically promised the Americans to sever relations between us and the Palestinians. Last but not least, the Gulf countries were pushing Saddam Hussein toward peace. They had even offered us $20 billion and then later $50 billion in reparations, in exchange for peace.

IRAQI CONCESSIONS

In this context, diplomatic missions followed one another in rapid succession. In early May, General Zia ul-Rahman, the late president of Bangladesh, and Habib Shatti returned with a message from Saddam Hussein. I went to the airport to welcome them. On the highway to the presidential palace they were amazed by the support the crowds demonstrated for me. During our first working meeting, Zia ul-Rahman spoke for over five hours. The translator suggested several times that I tell him that we were not there to beat around the bush. Then, suddenly, Zia ul-Rahman turned to me and said, "You've won."

"Won what?" I asked.

"Peace," he answered. He then explained that he had asked Saddam Hussein point blank whether he was ready to withdraw his forces unconditionally. Saddam Hussein's first response was "maybe," but the ensuing discussion changed it to "certainly."

Saddam Hussein had agreed on the following points: a fact-finding commission to determine responsibility for the conflict could be appointed even before the war ended, the ceasefire and the withdrawal of forces would occur simultaneously, and Iraq would honor the Algiers Agreement. I did not regret my patience.

Evidence that the goodwill was spreading came immediately after the departure of these heads of state. Four foreign affairs ministers from the nonaligned countries—Cuba, India, Zambia, and Palestine—showed up with new proposals. A form of rivalry developed between the Islamic countries and the nonaligned countries to see who could negotiate the peace. This competition seemed very healthy to me. Fidel Castro, leader of the nonaligned countries that year, declared himself ready to do anything necessary to help us. If he negotiated the peace, it would be good for him, good for the nonaligned countries, and good for Latin America's struggle against American imperialism.

These ministers proposed the same thing as the heads of state of the Islamic Conference, with one addition: they had extracted a promise that during this period of investigation and political negotiation we would each withdraw our forces several kilometers behind the lines, leaving a buffer zone between us to prevent clashes. I thought that this was a better, more complete proposal. I called a meeting of the Supreme Defense Council. Rajai kept insisting that continuing the war would solve all our problems. All the other members of the Council realized that we did not have the resources to continue fighting, the army chief of staff most of all. We therefore approved the proposals of the nonaligned countries. The behavior of Rajai and the mullahs who preferred an Iranian defeat to a Bani-Sadr victory reminded me of an old Persian legend. The wife of Sultan Mohamad Kharazmshah had caused a Mongol invasion because her men had killed Chinese merchants to seize their property. Court officials came to see her to suggest allowing her son, Jalal Eddine—a brave and courageous man—to become king in order to defuse the situation. She refused categorically, saying that she would rather be a slave of the Mongols than leave the throne and be content with the role of queen mother. Her stubbornness led to disaster and she did become a slave of the Mongols. At the end of her life, she ate scraps from the king's table but continued to say that she still preferred her current situation to that of ceding the throne to her son.

I went to see Khomeini the next day. By chance, some mullahs getting out of a couple of buses in front of his house began shouting when they saw me, "War! War until victory!" Who had informed them? It was a mystery to me. I had decided to be resolute in presenting the Supreme Defense Council's decision to

•

148

Khomeini so that he would accept Saddam Hussein's proposals. Actually, he had no choice, but he asked me not to talk about peace because of the clerics. I became angry and said that these same results could have been achieved after only two months of war, that it had dragged on only because of the mullahs, and that if they wanted to continue the slaughter, it was their business, but I was going to explain the details of the peace plan to the people. He relented, and as I was leaving he said, "Talk about peace; do whatever you want!"

The end of the war was approaching. The United States would have to choose between normal, official relations with a democratic state and shady dealings with the mullahs. I had no doubt what its choice would be. My conviction was borne out when I read an article in the *New York Times* stating that because of the hostage affair the United States government wanted very much to destroy the Iranian revolution, but not Iran. At the same time, Henry Kissinger wrote that the revolution in Iran had to be crushed regardless of the cost; otherwise, it would be the end of U.S. influence in the region.

The budget submitted by the Rajai government in early May told me all I needed to know about the posture of the United States. The total was $45 billion, $15 billion higher than the budget we had prepared after the Shah's departure. It included $35 billion in oil sales, or 3.5 million barrels a day.

I issued a statement warning the public that this budget went along with Reagan's policy of smashing prices and regaining control of OPEC, especially since Saudi Arabia had decided to increase production. This excess production was a splendid gift to the Americans.

Since Rajai was preaching a policy of total austerity, what was the purpose of this budget if not to buy arms and continue the war? I requested a debate on the budget and they consented, knowing that I could mention neither the agreement with the United States nor arms purchases without the army and the Revolutionary Guards jumping down my throat. The debate centered on continuation of the war and included a general evaluation of the budget, which, as far as I was concerned, meant total dependence on foreign powers. We recorded this debate, but because I was forced from office it was never broadcast. I

•

organized a secret meeting with the military to explain that they were the first victims of this new budget. They were as yet unaware that the allocations to the Guards and other revolutionary organizations were four times greater than theirs—a clear indication of what fate held in store for the regular army.

Despite this war-oriented budget, I had enjoyed considerable political, military, and diplomatic successes during this period. In particular, we had forced Saddam Hussein to accept peace on our terms because he felt that he was losing, even though his army still occupied part of Iran. In May and June 1981 it would not have been an exaggeration to say that we had won a political victory.

This success, plus unprecedented popularity, made me a bigger target than ever.

15

KHOMEINI UNDECIDED

UNDER THE CIRCUMSTANCES, ONLY KHOMEINI COULD FORCE me from office. My popularity protected me from Beheshti and the others. The Imam himself had become the prize in the contest between the mullahs and me. They tried very hard to bring him into their camp and keep him there, while I did everything I could to prevent him from permanently siding with them. My only hope of winning was to fight fiercely to preserve the basic freedoms.

We were on the verge of civil war because the revolutionary organizations and the mullahs were now resorting to terrorist acts. No longer content with disrupting meetings, they were attacking or arresting people in the streets. Torture became a common practice. In a speech, I violently denounced this odious behavior. Khomeini tried to smooth things over by forming a committee to investigate the "rumor" of torture. I personally gave him 400 photos of torture victims, as well as films and documents implicating the Guards, the committees, and the revolutionary tribunals. There was no doubt. Residents of Ghazvin went to see a member of this committee, Montazeri's son Mohamad, to request that he observe the brutality in the city's prison. He did nothing and even stated publicly that they were idiots because they did not know that the committee had actually been instructed by the Imam to conclude that there was no torture.

Another member of this committee, Besharati—now secretary of state for foreign affairs—came to tell me that the situation in the prisons was worse than anyone could imagine, but that he was nevertheless going to sign the report denying the torture. I asked him how he could sleep at night after such an act of cowardice.

One day at my home, with several deputies present, I was visited by a young student from Tabriz who said that he had been tortured with cigarettes. He explained that the Guards had taken him into a house and had written the word *Beheshti* on his chest with cigarettes. One of the deputies present, who had himself been tortured with cigarettes during the Shah's reign, examined him and said that he was telling the truth. Khomeini's son-in-law, Eshraghi, was also present. After the student left, Eshraghi claimed that he was a member of the Mujahedeen and that he had burned himself in order to slander the regime. I advised him not to make such excuses for what he had just seen, because it was slandering the regime to suggest that a young man was prepared to mutilate himself to harm our cause. He did not change his mind, however, and he told the same story to Khomeini, who repeated it verbatim on the radio. I wrote to Khomeini, telling him that it would be better for the regime to admit that certain organizations were torturing people and to put a stop to it.

I realized that the mullahs' problem was no longer one of separating the people from their president, but of neutralizing the people, especially the young. They were not their only targets. The mullahs openly attacked any clerics who disagreed with them. Important leaders such as Ghoumi and Rabani Shirazy—members of the Council of Guardians of the Constitution, appointed by Khomeini—were mistreated as well as supporters of the Imam, simply because they disagreed with the Islamic Republic Party. They also terrorized journalists, some of whom stopped publishing their newspapers. By this time, there were only two newspapers not under their control: Bazargan's and ours. They banned Bazargan's paper and arrested the editor. We launched a campaign to defend freedom of the press and the people paid a great deal of money into an account to help bring the newspaper back. We conducted a public opinion poll on this

•

subject. An overwhelming majority of those polled were against the suppression of newspapers; only 12 percent thought that the measure was fair. Khomeini called these polls seditious.

The clerics were also at work undermining the army, where they were interfering more and more, especially Montazeri, who had appropriated the services of an officer I had relieved of command of the army, Sayad Shirazi. Montazeri sent him to the radio and television stations, meetings, and Friday prayers to launch attacks against me. Although he was detested in the army, he was rewarded after my departure by being named commander of the army. Except for Shirazi and a few members of the Tudeh Party, all of whom were later shot, the clerics failed to gain a foothold in the army. Generally speaking, the military refused to play the mullahs' game, especially after the reorganization. The principle of freedom in the army was respected, and even if all the commanders and superior officers obeyed the Imam's orders, it was no longer blind obedience.

Khomeini often pressured me through his son or son-in-law to praise the revolutionary organizations publicly, but I refused to shower praises on those who would soon—I knew—become the instruments of my own death and the executioners of the revolution! The organizations were created to enforce the law; it was not the law's duty to bow to their demands. They no longer hesitated to state publicly that the interests of these organizations took precedence over everything.

This principle still stands since Mousavi Khoeiniha, the Supreme Court prosecutor, later said that he was no ultra-legalist and that he would never sacrifice the interests of the oppressed to observance of the law. I, on the other hand, acknowledged "absolute priority of the law" because I knew that law-abiding citizens cannot remain neutral in the event of a coup d'état. In Third World countries, the architects of a coup always begin by trampling on the laws to impose their own rule.

WAR BY OPINION POLL

During the months of April and May 1981, we conducted a series of public opinion polls. Since we were muzzled ourselves, we decided to let the people speak. Enormous samples were chosen for these polls, sometimes including as many as 10,000 people. The polls covered a wide variety of subjects, ranging from home life to the status of women after the revolution as well as everyday problems, the hostage affair, and the popularity of political figures. This last poll had been conducted twice a month for more than six months to gauge how the people reacted to our daily quarrels. The people's concerns were edifying: 35.7 percent of those polled placed economic difficulties at the top of their list of concerns; among women, this figure climbed to 56.4 percent. Next on the list were internal political problems (censorship, the drift toward dictatorship, daily obstacles created by the mullahs) with a 27 percent score, and in third place was the war, with a score of only 8.8 percent. What struck me most was the changing status of women in society, even though all political activity at the decision-making level was normally denied them on religious grounds. Their participation in the various elections was astonishing: 30 percent in the parliamentary elections for the vote on constitutional law; 74.4 percent and 90 percent in the presidential elections. Once liberated from religious strictures, Iranian women considered themselves full-fledged citizens. Unfortunately, all that their involvement meant was that the gap between theory and practice had grown a little smaller. I knew it would take a long time for behavior to catch up with the change in attitude, not to mention the resistance of social structures.

Mahdavi-Khani, the interior minister, launched his own series of public opinion polls to counteract ours. He used an even larger sample, but the results did not live up to his expectations because they confirmed my findings almost point for point. The people, for example, were against the Islamic Republic Party's attempts to seize power, proving me right in consequence. Finally, concerning the hostage affair, 92 percent of those polled thought that it was concluded in a manner beneficial to the United States and not Iran.

Khomeini, ever the shrewd politician, quickly realized that he had nothing to gain from this contest and ordered the minister to stop, claiming that he did not believe in opinion polls because the people were incapable of forming an opinion. It was hard for me to understand how this man, who had become a leader as the

•

result of a great popular movement, could speak of his people with such contempt. I attached great importance to the polls because they provided me with information about the status of our society and my own personal future. I followed the progress of our popularity ratings very closely. Although at the beginning of my presidency and until the late 1980s, Khomeini was always in first place, far ahead of me, for several weeks the trend had reversed itself until there was a very wide margin in my favor. In the last poll, the difference was more than 25 points. Eric Rouleau was in my office when these statistics were brought in. I showed them to him and asked him not to publish them. Seventy-six percent of the those polled were satisfied with Bani-Sadr, and only 49.5 percent with Khomeini. Among young people, the gap was even wider: 30 to 35 percent for Khomeini, 80 percent for Bani-Sadr. Rouleau did not publish the figures when he returned to Paris, but he did write in *Le Monde* that Bani-Sadr's popularity greatly surpassed that of Khomeini. Imagine his anger when he read the international press review he received each day! In any case, this article did not make much difference; the break between us was becoming irreparable.

KHOMEINI AND BANI-SADR AT CROSS PURPOSES

Near the end, I began an indirect dialogue with Khomeini. Actually, it was more of a monologue carried on through my daily column in the newspaper. I attacked him indirectly, for example, in book reviews. I happened to mention a work on Napoleon Bonaparte, written by a Russian and translated into Farsi. I commented at length on the day when the people of Paris turned out to hail their emperor on his departure for Saint Helena. Standing before the roaring crowd, he commented, "What a shame! Too often, I forgot about the real people." The real people were the workers, the peasants, the ordinary townspeople. At this very moment, the nervous middle classes were waiting impatiently for the conquering armies to enter Paris. They preferred a foreign army within their walls to workers marching in the suburbs.

I wanted Khomeini to understand that he was going to

sacrifice all of the people for a handful of mullahs and a few rich merchants, and that he was in danger of one day finding himself in Napoleon's position, abandoned by these same rich people who would oust him if it was in their interest. I also quoted the writings of Mossadegh: "A statesman must be courageous, must have a businessman's flair for taking risks, must know how to make sacrifices and timely decisions." I said that politicians faithful to these basic principles were rare in Iran, especially in this decadent century.

In this column I related an anecdote that raised my opposition to Khomeini another notch. I told of a visit to the front in Khousistan, where, in a very exposed position, I had seen a female donkey lying on the ground, killed by a shell. Beside her stood her colt, his eyes riveted on his mother despite the noise and the shells falling all around him. For what seemed an eternity, I watched this animal whose devotion to his mother made him oblivious to all danger. I used this story to denounce violence in all its forms, war in particular. Khomeini telephoned to say that I was a good writer, but perhaps it was not wise, in the midst of war, to make propaganda against violence. I asked him if he loved force. He replied, "Yes, it is necessary."

I became furious because his role as a spiritual leader was not to encourage hatred and violence, but love of one's neighbor. He replied, "You want me to be a pope, to be content with uttering a few pretty words from time to time to please everyone." Our tempers flared, and I accused him of behaving like a medieval pope.

Our relationship had deteriorated to such an extent that I called together a few friends to analyze the situation, to make the president's coordinating offices (somewhat like support committees) more active, and to shield them from the repressive organizations. Our objective was to prevent Khomeini from taking action against us. Certain individuals recommended attacking him directly to dispel the myth and finish him once and for all. Others said that a confrontation between Bani-Sadr and Khomeini was to be avoided at all costs. Still others thought that the attack should be delayed and that the mullahs, hobbled by the agreement with the Americans, would find no opportunity of carrying it out. As time went on, the Americans would be forced to accept official relations at the government level. Unfortunately, we chose the latter solution: temporizing.

Like several of my friends, I deluded myself about Khomeini's willingness to go all the way, that is, to fire on the people if necessary. I could not imagine it since, historically, the Shiite clergy have almost always sided with the people against the established power. We thought that Khomeini would continue harrassing me but that he would not attempt any definitive action against me, his spiritual son, Iran's first president, elected in accordance with a constitution approved by him. What a mistake that was! I have rarely discussed this subject since leaving Iran because I never stopped hoping that he would turn back, and I wanted to give him a chance to correct this error. I wanted him to admit his mistakes and to renounce totalitarianism.

I believed in popular support, which was real. Even among the Revolutionary Guards I gained some ground. They saw that we had recovered 40 percent of our territory and that we were about to score a political victory. Naturally wanting to be on the winning side, some of the Guards wrote to me, expressing their support despite the prohibitions. Moreover, many officials in the clerics' party had begun to fear the size of the popular movement. In the province of Khorassan, for example, the governor was beaten for not announcing my arrival. The prefects, who represented the government and were in daily contact with the people, were so hated that they wanted to quit their jobs. By contrast, everywhere I went—in every city and in every village— the people rejoiced. The same slogans were heard everywhere; the collective consciousness expressed itself spontaneously. I was urged to resist the mullahs who "are robbing us of our revolution and endangering our country." I knew the slogans by heart: "Down with the three crooks!" "Bani-Sadr, we support you!" One day, as I was coming into the city of Khoramabad, a young boy marked the windows of my car with his own blood to demonstrate his solidarity and that of his city with my cause.

Despite the blitz of photographs and meetings, despite the intimidation and repression, the mullahs sensed that they were being increasingly rejected by the people. They could no longer attend meetings or rallies; they had become virtual prisoners in their own homes. I pressed my advantage even further by making

Khomeini agree to reopen the universities, which was another failure for the Islamic Republic Party.

A group of deputies came to tell me of their concern. According to them, we were already living in a dictatorship since the newspapers were shutting down, public meetings were becoming increasingly difficult to organize, and in parliament everyone was keeping quiet because of the ever-present threat. They told me of their intention to send a letter to Rafsanjani, the head of parliament, to tell him that they would refuse to attend the sessions if freedoms were not restored. I expressed my support, while at the same time warning them that their resistance might cost them their lives.

A short time later, I met with a group of representatives from the Bazaar, who assured me of their support but reproached me for not having warned them sooner. Since things were going well for me politically and militarily, I told Rajai that he had no business being prime minister, that he was useless except as a weapon against me, that if the war were lost because of his friends the mullahs, history would never forgive him, and that the judgment of God, in whom he believed, would be terrible. Shaken, he said he was ready to resign the next morning. He did no such thing, of course, but this story shows how little confidence he had.

I realized that things could still go either way. The public, some of the Guards, and the army were on my side. Against me were parliament, the Council of Guardians of the Constitution, the government, and the Islamic Republic Party.

I sensed that Khomeini was undecided, pulled in several directions.

Some members of the Society of Combatant Clergymen of Tehran—supporters of Khomeini but hostile to Beheshti and Rafsanjani—came to see me to report on a conversation that they had had with the Imam about me. They had asked him the following question, point-blank: "Tell us, is Bani-Sadr a threat to Islam, to Iran? He answered no categorically, adding that I was sincere, courageous, capable, that he loved me dearly, even though I sometimes said things embarrassing to the regime. This confirmed what he had said to the heads of state of the Islamic Conference in an official speech: "Learn from our president how to win the hearts of the people."

•

I wrote him a long letter explaining in detail my plan for victory in four months; then I moved onto higher ground. I expressed my ambitions for our revolution, which could have marked—and might yet mark—the end of dependent relationships and the dawn of equitable relations between states, without superpower interference. It would be the end of dictatorships and the beginning of coordinated development, at least in the Muslim countries. I added, "This is the role that you, Khomeini, can play by proving it possible to reconcile science and faith, art and faith, politics and faith, freedom and faith, progress and faith—which would become the spirit of every movement."

Without my realizing it, this letter had the effect of revealing to Khomeini all of his regrets; he became instantly aware of the enormity of his failure. Moreover, as an officer later told me, the four-month period I mentioned sealed my fate. I had to be eliminated before the war was won.

16

REMOVAL FROM OFFICE OR COUP D'ÉTAT

IN EARLY JUNE, PARLIAMENT PASSED TWO BILLS: ONE suppressing the powers of the president and the other allowing the government to appoint ministers without presidential approval, a measure wholly contrary to constitutional law. Khomeini, circumvented by two members of the Council of Guardians of the Constitution, did nothing. They had convinced him that his intervention would weaken parliament. This was a curious step since the Council, neutral by definition, is supposed to uphold the Constitution. I counterattacked immediately by calling a press conference to propose a referendum. The people would settle the difference between the president and parliament. To the question of whether I would resign, I categorically answered no. This was too much for Khomeini, who attacked me publicly for the first time. "This is not the Mossadegh era; a referendum is out of the question." The day after this outburst I was scheduled to go to Shiraz to award medals to pilots who had flown more than fifty missions since the beginning of the war. Colonel Fakouri, the defense minister, asked me if I still planned to go. "Of course! He can criticize me if he wants to. We shall see how the people react!" I was not wrong. There was a huge crowd at the Shiraz air base, shouting, weeping, totally supportive. An extraordinary demonstration!

The pace of events quickened. On June 5, accompanied by Eric Rouleau, the French journalist, I went on an inspection tour in the eastern section of the country, in Baluchistan. Upon arriving in Zahedan, the provincial capital, an enormous crowd was waiting for me. Nevertheless, in the presidential election I had won only 21 percent of the vote in that area. The welcome was so enthusiastic that Rouleau wrote, "It is a plebiscite! What can Khomeini do against that?"

This plebiscite was my undoing. The Imam could not tolerate such a show of support when the people had that very morning ignored the ceremonies he had organized to commemorate the massacre of June 6, 1963. On returning to Tehran, I met with my advisers to develop a strategy in response to Khomeini's position. We concluded that a direct confrontation was still out of the question, so I decided to visit him on June 6 to try to effect a reconciliation.

He received me in a very friendly manner, in top form, making little jokes. We discussed the situation in the eastern region of the country, the Afghan refugee problem, the four military operations in preparation in case I failed to win a political victory. The objective of this plan, which he had approved concurrently with the Supreme Defense Council, was victory in the field before the end of the first year of the war.

I had no idea that he had at the same time summoned the military and the Guards to plan my removal from office. As I was leaving, I upbraided his son, accusing him of betraying his father by announcing on the radio that millions of people had attended the previous day's commemoration. "Tell your father the truth! Tell him that we're hearing 'Down with Khomeini' here and there. Everyone knows what's going on; we have to get back to the principles of the revolution quickly."

He pretended to agree with me, then insisted that I work with Beheshti, Rafsanjani, and the others. I reminded him once more of the agreement with Reagan, which they had no more intention of renouncing than they did of stepping aside to let competent individuals take their place. We had nothing more to say to each other.

I went to Hamadan, my birthplace. The crowd shouted, "Down with Beheshti! Down with the three crooks!" Hamadan was the first city to close the local branch of the Islamic Republic Party. All the way from the airport to my parents' home, where I was to have lunch, I heard the same slogans.

The response was not slow in coming. At 2:00 P.M., the radio announced that the prosecutor of the revolutionary court had halted the publication of my newspaper. At 4:00 P.M., I gave a very forceful speech. "Just how far do you plan to go with your attacks on freedom? I can no longer remain silent."

The next day, Khomeini publicly endorsed the prosecutor's decision. He ended his speech with this sentence: "I will break pens and I will shut mouths. . . ."

From Hamadan, I went to the front at Kermanshah and wrote a long letter to the Imam. Over the telephone, his nephew read me the answer, which began, "I love you like a son. I have done everything I can to protect you." He then proposed settling the problem with the government on three conditions: dismiss those of my aides who annoyed the mullahs, suppress five or six parties such as the Mujahedeen and the Fedayeen-e-Khalq, and recognize the legality of parliament, the Supreme Judicial Council, the Council of Guardians of the Constitution, and the government.

My answer was an unqualified no. I could never approve this parliament, constituted through fraudulent elections, or this Supreme Judicial Council, the members of which are appointed arbitrarily. All forms of dictatorship have been tried in the world: Marxist dictatorships, fascism, Latin American military dictatorships, Nasser-type dictatorships, Algerian types, and so on. All have failed. Let's not follow these catastrophic examples. Let's try to reestablish true democracy in Iran, modeled on that which existed in the time of the Prophet: freedom of speech, freedom of thought, freedom of consultation, human rights.

The Imam's response can be summed up in a few words: "I will no longer read Bani-Sadr's letters!"

THE LEGALISTIC ARMY

The army chief of staff, accompanied by several officers, came to see me at 5:00 P.M. on June 7. For the second time, he proposed

•

military intervention. He did not consider this initiative a military coup since the people were with us. For him, it was only a matter of putting an end to an attempt at religious totalitarianism. I did not agree with this proposal, but to remove all doubt, we discussed how many units would be necessary to seize power. It would take two divisions, and we only had two batallions in Tehran. We would therefore have to withdraw troops from the front and negotiate with the Iraqis to prevent them from taking advantage of the situation. We estimated that it would take over a month to complete the operation, whereas a coup, to be successful, must be executed in two hours. The plan was unrealistic without decapitating the regime by eliminating Beheshti, Rafsanjani, and Khomeini himself. It seems that others had considered this possibility before us. In any case, I did not give my consent.

That very evening, at 11:30, a statement from Khomeini was read on the radio. One sentence sealed my fate: "Bani-Sadr is no longer commander in chief of the armed forces."

The Imam was surely not very happy with himself. When the statement was read, he was already asleep, since he goes to bed every evening at precisely 10:00 P.M.

On the morning of the eighth, I returned to Tehran. The chief of staff and the commander of the army warned me that they had been summoned by Khomeini, who was undoubtedly going to offer them my position, at least temporarily. The entire Tehran air base gave me a rousing welcome. In a short speech, I insisted that I would resist dictatorship.

At my office, I received a telephone call from Khomeini's son-in-law, who told me that the Imam, informed of the crowd and the speech at the air base, would take whatever steps were necessary if I did not keep quiet. Another clergyman, Lahouti, also came to warn me because Rafsanjani had let him know in no uncertain terms that I was courting death if I did not obey. To make my position regarding the army perfectly clear, I had the following message read to all units: "Your duty is to remain faithful to your commitment to the country. You must not interfere in internal politics. You must defend your country against the aggressor."

Ahmed Khomeini tried one last time to effect a reconciliation through Shirazy, the son of a religious leader. I was asked to sign an agreement with Khomeini; failing that, according to his son Ahmed, the Imam was capable of anything in the name of Islam. I stood my ground. He had declared war; I accepted it.

On June 12, I had one of the deputies read a statement in parliament in which I said that the war would continue, that it would consume the Iranian and Iraqi armed forces, and that it would enable the United States to achieve its goal of hegemony over the region. History has proved me right. As with the hostage affair—ended in defeat—the war would continue until Iran was humiliated. The leaders would then say that there was no alternative but to accept peace, even a dishonorable one. I concluded by informing the deputies that four ministers from the nonaligned countries were supposed to have arrived on June 8 to propose a peace plan advantageous to us, but that their trip had been postponed *sine die* because of events, causing us to lose our last chance of victory.

In the meantime, I had met with my advisers. At times, I imagined myself removed from office, called before a revolutionary tribunal, sentenced to death. I told myself that, after all, history would decide who was right and who was wrong. My wife especially urged me to resist, reminding me that for the people, I embodied the revolution as much as—if not more than— Khomeini. I had never imagined that it would come to this. We had not even arranged for a place to hide.

We developed a plan to act in coordination with the people. Contrary to what was said later, I never ordered the Mujahedeen to decapitate the regime. To resist, I had the thirty people in my personal guard. How could a city be taken with such a small contingent? We thought that if the people joined us, we could turn the situation to our advantage. An initial mobilization effort failed.

We wanted the Bazaar to go on strike, the merchants to draw their blinds, the people to assemble, and for everyone to march together to parliament, to the prime minister's office, and to the palace of justice. This is how we wanted to strike the leaders of the regime. It was not a question of killing or bombing, but only of removing from power those who prevented enforcement of the laws.

The Bazaar's lack of organization killed the plan.

•

A second effort was made on June 15. The National Front had decided to organize a demonstration to support me. A representative of the Mujahedeen came to inform me that there would be *seven thousand* armed men in the march, ready to support me. I knew this to be impossible since the Mujahedeen had no more than seven hundred members in Tehran.

At 2:00 P.M. a statement from Khoemini was broadcast on the radio, outlawing all members of the National Front. At 3:00 Bazargan read a statement of submission, thus dissociating himself from the demonstration. A group of friends came to tell me that the people had assembled, that Khomeini's men were also there, armed with clubs, and that no leader of the National Front was to be found. How could I participate in a demonstration when its organizers refused to come?

The people were confused. My presence might have turned the whole thing into a bloodbath. I therefore decided to have nothing further to do with this ill-prepared project. I responded to Khomeini's demand that I criticize myself on television by sending him a strongly-worded telegram accusing him of treason. My isolation was reinforced by the fact that the presidential coordinating offices had just been ransacked.

UNDERGROUND

On the evening of June 15 I went into hiding. In the next few days, I sent two messages to the Imam, one written, the other recorded. In the first, I begged Khomeini to halt the establishment of a dictatorship and not to sacrifice the country in order that a few traitors might govern Iran. In the second message, I recounted at length the difficult moments when the army was disorganized and the Iraqis were seriously threatening us, before we had attained our current position of strength. I urged him to remain vigilant and to execute the four military operations designed to end the war as quickly as possible, inasmuch as a political conclusion to the conflict was no longer possible.

In hiding at the home of friends in central Tehran, I followed events from day to day. On June 20, a large demonstration in support of the president was organized. The Mujahedeen

•

participated, although on June 15 they had not budged. What they actually wanted was to use my popularity for their own purposes. Until noon, the crowd shouted, "Long live Bani-Sadr; we will protect you." The people waved placards with my picture on them, but then, gradually, photos of Rajavi, the leader of the Mujahedeen, replaced mine. The crowd, feeling deceived, dispersed.

The same day, the Guards provoked armed skirmishes. This was the prelude to repression. That evening, fifty people were dragged before a firing squad. In the following days, the numbers increased: 100, 150, 200, 300, 400, 500, even children only 8 years of age! Participation in a demonstration was sufficient reason for being assassinated. Families were not even warned. It was at this moment that I realized the enormity of my error: Khomeini was indeed capable of ordering executions and firing on the people.

Hiding in the apartment of a member of the Iranian Nation Party, I heard a terrible explosion on June 28. The headquarters of the Islamic Republic Party had been blown up. Someone called me immediately to tell me that Beheshti and over a hundred others had been killed. I issued a statement strongly condemning the attack. My associates could not understand why I condemned an attack on those who had destroyed the revolution and plunged our country into war. I did it because I thought that if we had resisted the first executions of the Shah's men, in the name of the principles of the revolution, we might not be where we were.

The regime gave several versions of this explosion. Members of the Mujahedeen came to see me the next day and told me that they had had nothing to do with it. In the following days, I tried to find out who had organized the coup. According to the information I obtained, it was the work of an extremely capable expert, no ordinary terrorist, who, working on the inside with time and connections, had developed such a sophisticated device that no one could detect it or escape the explosion. But on whose behalf? There was talk of the Revolutionary Guards, the army, some secret organization. After he left Iran, Rajavi claimed responsibility for the attack on behalf of the Mujahedeen. He justified his earlier denial by citing security reasons. I myself thought that the attack had been planned and executed from within the Islamic Republic Party.

•

During his visit the day following the explosion, Rajavi proposed an alliance. He offered to place the Mujahedeen at my disposal. I explained my reservations about his movement's respect for the freedom of others. He was, however, known for his anti-imperialism (according to certain recent surveys, the American victims of terrorism in Iran during the Shah's reign were not killed by the Mujahedeen, as was believed, but by their own government because they knew too much). We also discussed justice—there was no point in replacing the tribunals of the mullahs with those of the Mujahedeen—and ideology, to find a way of reconciling Islam and Marxism. I suggested a trial alliance, and on June 29 I secretly moved to their quarters.

There was one explosion after another in this period. In August 1981, the prime minister's office was blown up, killing the new president of the Republic, Rajai, and his prime minister, Bahonar. This attack was the work of an ordinary terrorist.

A short time later, the airplane carrying the chief of staff and commander of the air force exploded in flight. For a long time, the regime blamed the Mujahedeen, but then a doubt surfaced in parliament, the right accusing the minister of industry, Nabavi, and his party, the Combatants of the Islamic Revolution, of being responsible for these two operations. Several members of this party were arrested, and two of them were even tortured. According to another version, the bombings were the work of the Tudeh Communist Party. In fact, with Soviet help, the Tudeh Party could organize anything it wanted to.

Several hundred top secret telexes from the CIA were among the tons of documents seized by students of the Imam's line when hostages were taken at the U.S. embassy in Tehran.

The Americans who took the time to shred most of these documents never imagined that the students would carefully reconstruct each of these telexes (see pp. 171–72).

One of them is a memorandum concerning Abol Hassan Bani-Sadr, designated by the CIA code name L/I.

Following is an exact translation:

Positive

•

2. Although he probably has no financial problems at the moment, he has to bear in mind that he could be exiled with little notice and could need financial support at that time.

Negative

3. Experience over the years tends to emphasize the tendency of newspaper publishers to be self-seeking and often unreliable. His decision to start up a newspaper may indicate that L/I is concerned only with his own political future and is not about to cooperate with us along the lines we envision.

These two excerpts were published by the mullahs. They faked the translation to prove that Bani-Sadr had contacts with the CIA and could be bought.

Much later, another version propagated by Rafsanjani made the rounds. It blamed the Medhi Hashemi group for the attack on the military officials. This is arguable since Rafsanjani is the sworn enemy of Montazeri, Hashemi's protector.

In short, each time the regime wanted to eliminate some group, this accusation resurfaced. While I was still in hiding somewhere in Iran, the royalist radio broadcast a story claiming that I had told a reporter that I had documents proving the existence of the mullahs' agreement with the United States. Consequently, the mullahs were extremely frightened and looked everywhere for me. Nabavi said in an interview that I would not be harmed if I turned over the documents. To discredit me, they published a letter proving that I was a spy for the Americans. This letter was published without a translation, a simplistic maneuver enabling them to make it say whatever they wanted since very few Iranians can read English. And who would have dared to risk censure by saying that this document proved, on the contrary, that neither I nor my friends were willing to cooperate with the CIA? (See preceding page.) This document later proved to be very useful. It confirmed my integrity, and I used it as a weapon against Khomeiniism and Reaganism. I explained how the United States tried to corrupt Third World leaders. They did not succeed with me, but they must have obtained satisfaction from a great many others!

Had they been able to get their hands on me after the

publication of this letter, I would have been summarily executed as an agent of the United States. They looked for me everywhere, steadily increasing the pressure to find me, especially since I continued addressing the people through the press.

According to constitutional law, elections were to be held within forty days of my removal from office. They wasted no time. This election was of the greatest importance to me because if the people voted in large numbers, it would mean that they approved my elimination. If they stayed away, however, I could still consider myself their president and it would be my duty to fulfill this role within the limits of my responsibilities in order that democracy might one day be restored in Iran. I had a statement published explaining this view of the elections.

Rajavi cared little for public opinion in this election. This sign of contempt for democracy led to our first dispute. The very evening of the election, one of the election observers informed us that only 2.7 million people had voted, meaning that 90 percent of the population had stayed away from the polls. The people, then, had shunned this travesty, which consisted of nominating three candidates from the same party for the sole purpose of having Rajai elected. However, he was not to enjoy his new duties for long since, as mentioned above, he was killed in a bomb blast three weeks after his election.

A week later, I agreed to leave the country with Rajavi to continue the struggle abroad. I put on a military uniform and then some members of Rajavi's organization drove me, after dark, to Freedom Square in Tehran. We broke the fast—it was the month of Ramadan—and then we went to the military base. No one recognized me. We waited on the runway until 11:00 P.M. Rajavi arrived and we got into a cargo plane, which took us out of Iran via Turkey. At the border, the pilot contacted the office of the French prime minister, Pierre Mauroy, to request permission to land in France. Mauroy consented, and we flew straight to a military base here in France. Another period of exile was beginning for me.

I hesitated a long time before leaving my country, and then I realized that there are many ways of fighting a dictatorship. Mossadegh had his method; Allende had his. I chose to leave so that I might state my case to the American public and to the world.

•

I did not leave to wage a political battle to regain power, nor to escape danger, but to expose Khomeiniism and its innate ties to Reaganism.

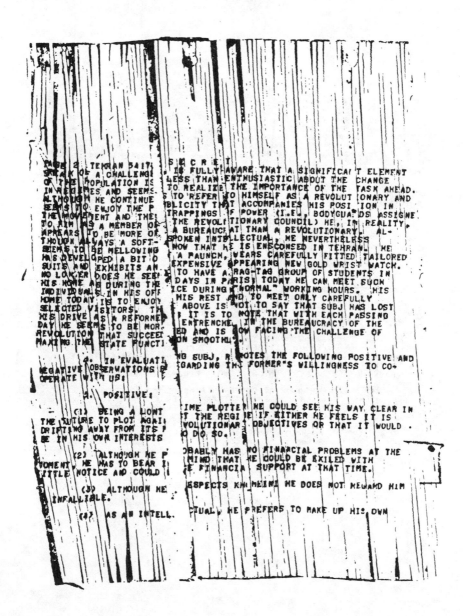

PAGE 3 TEHRAN 5417 S E C R E T
MIND RATHER THAN TO FOLLOW ANOTHER BLINDLY.

(5) HE IS A APE THAT CLIQUES ARE DEVELOPING WITHIN THE
REGIME AND IS PROBABLY AWARE THAT HE MUST BE CAUTIOUS IN DEALING
WITH THOSE AROUND HIM . FOR EXAMPLE, HE STATED THAT ALL MEMBERS
OF THE REVOLUTIONARY COUNCIL ARE NOT EQUALLY COMPETENT BUT THAT
HE HAS TO LIVE AND DE AL WITH THEM. THIS UNCERTAINTY WILL PROBABLY
CAUSE HIM TO KEEP A F W DOORS OPEN.

(6) HE HAS P LITICAL AMBITION. HE PROBABLY STARTED HIS
NEWSPAPER IN ORDER O USE IT AS A POWER BASE FOR FUTURE POLITICAL
OBJECTIVES.

(7) ALTHOUGH PRESSED FOR TIME AT BUSY PERIODS IN PARIS
AND TEHRAN, HE HAS G N OUT OF HIS WAY TO MEET US. R COMMENT
WISH TO NOTE THAT HI VAILABILITY REMAINS A PROBLEM FROM OUR
POINT OF VIEW.)

B. NEGATIVE.

(1) BEING FIRM ENTRENCHED IN THE PRESENT REGIME, SUBJ
REALLY DOES NOT NEED S AT THE MOMENT.

(2) DISCLOSURE OF A CLANDESTINE RELATIONSHIP WITH US
WOULD PROBABLY END SUBJ POLITICAL CAREER. IT IS CERTAIN THAT
HE WILL NOT OVERLOOK T POINT.

(3) EXPERIENCE OVER THE YEARS TENDS TO EMPHASIZE THE
TENDENCY OF NEWSPAPER U ISHERS TO BE SELF-SEEKING AND OFTEN
UNRELIABLE. HIS DECISI TO START UP A NEWSPAPER MAY INDICATE
THAT L/1 IS CONCERNED O WITH HIS OWN POLITICAL FUTURE AND IS
NOT ABOUT TO COOPERATE H US ALONG THE LINES WE ENVISION.

(4) ALTHOUGH S E S COMMENTS AGAINST U.S. FIRMS MEDDLING
IN THE INTERNAL AFFAIRS O IRAN MAY HAVE BEEN A SIGNAL THAT HE
ANTS NOTHING TO DO WITH HE USG, R IS INCLINED TO THINK
HERWISE.

5. ON THE ASSUM 1 ON THAT OUR INTEREST IN RECRUITING L/1
TINUES, THE FOLLOWING S MMARIZES R'S THOUGHTS ON TWO POSSIBLE
ROACHES:

17

TOWARD PERPETUAL WAR

July 1981–July 1982

BEFORE LEAVING IRAN, I HAD WRITTEN A DOCUMENT approved by Rajavi. I set forth the principles to which we were both committed. The first concerned the war. We decided—and Rajavi was much more emphatic on this point than I—not to accept any rapprochement with the Iraqis. We then agreed not to accept any offer from the Americans, especially the CIA, and to fight against the royalists and counterrevolutionaries, who must not be allowed to take advantage of the situation. We knew that the royalists were planning to enter West Azerbaijan. Counter-revolutionaries on both the Left and the Right wanted to apply Lenin's slogan, "Take advantage of external war to overthrow the regime." In an August 1981 issue of *Le Figaro*, a journalist wrote about a rapprochement between the royalists and the Kurds. By incorporating the Kurds in our resistance movement, we put an end to that idea and prevented Iran from becoming another Lebanon, which would have been inevitable if the royalists and the Kurdish organizations had opened a second front and we had done the same. We also wanted to prevent the counterrevolu-tionaries from representing themselves as the only serious alternative by monopolizing the Western media for propaganda purposes.

Ever since Mossadegh, the Americans had been unable to take control of the opposition, even though, at the time, many opponents of the regime were American agents. Our success in this regard is demonstrated by the fact that, today, groups backed by the Soviet Union and the United States are no longer important; they discredited themselves by revealing their dependence, their weakness, and their corruption. We also wanted to make sure that the Soviets were not given an opportunity to infiltrate the regime through the Tudeh movement and the Fedayeen-e-Khalq, especially since these parties claimed to have been very active in my overthrow. We revealed here in Paris, for example, that a Soviet agent arrested in Iran had given the Americans a complete list of the Russian agents working in all the countries of the region. Except for the arms deals, this was the first specific collaboration between the Khomeini regime and the United States. This, then, was the main thrust of our activities in the early period of our exile.

Strangely, in August, September, and October 1981, Saddam Hussein failed to take advantage of all these upheavals—arrests, explosions, political struggles in Iran—to attack. He passed up this golden opportunity to finish us off for one simple reason. He had started the war with a green light from the United States, but he also knew that the United States would not accept our total defeat, as Carter had once informed us.

Although the external war was on the point of ending, within the country violence was wreaking havoc. Terrorism and executions proliferated, causing another brain drain. The revolutionary organizations, the Guards, the committees, and the revolutionary tribunals were ubiquitous in the cities, while the army sustained the initiative on the front, despite the fact that General Fallahi, the interim commander in chief of the armed forces appointed to replace me, was killed in the explosion of his airplane. The mullahs were at war with everyone. First, they attacked the Mujahedeen and my supporters, then they went after dissidents in their own party, and, finally they got rid of religious rebels such as the supporters of Ghotbzadeh and Shariatmadari. Ghotbzadeh was arrested while planning a coup with a group of military officers. Shariatmadari was placed under surveillance

•

and his associates were sent to prison. Ayatollah Shariatmadari would soon become the first religious leader in the history of Iran to be excommunicated.

After the attack on Beheshti, three factions emerged within the party. For simplicity's sake, it will suffice to say that there was a Right, a Left, and a center represented by Rafsanjani.

At the close of this period, Khomeini forbade the Revolutionary Guards to be members of a political party, his objective being to remove the Mujahedeen of the Islamic revolution from power before dissolving their movement.

In June 1982, after some of the very first revolutionaries and part of the clergy were eliminated, and after the new organizations were purged, totalitarian power became an established fact.

A RUDDERLESS ECONOMY

In this period, the economic picture was not promising. It was made worse by the policy of the mullahs, who sold off our oil and rejected the objectives defined while I was president: raising prices, building up our foreign exchange reserves for use as a weapon in the oil market, and capitalizing on the crisis in the industrialized countries to enforce a policy of development. Previously, the forces driving our economy—expertise, raw materials, capital—all went to the West. Now that the crisis was hitting the West and forcing its professionals and experts into unemployment, why wouldn't they come to work in our country? It would be a way of solving our respective problems, while at the same time permitting the harmonious development of mankind as a whole.

As soon as I left Iran, the government adopted the opposite policy and sharply cut oil prices. They gave in to pressure from the Americans, who wanted to force prices down at all costs, even though they had nearly confiscated $16 billion of our assets in the first two years of the revolution because of the hostages. The government even sold gold, which was the standard for our currency, and instead of utilizing the crisis in the West for development purposes, took advantage of it to buy arms.

While we wanted to put an end to war and insecurity, the

regime exported war and terrorism, thereby furthering the objectives of the Israelis and the Americans.

Since the beginning of the revolution, the oil economy had gone through three phases: at the very beginning, price increases; then, stagnation and a slight downward trend during the embargo; finally, a drop. In the same period, arms purchases had increased and Reagan's economic policy, based on low inflation and high interest rates, had drawn all foreign exchange to the United States. I therefore predicted a strong dollar that would benefit financial brokers and the U.S. economy, but not oil producers. This could be considered a sort of tax, paid by Japan and Europe to the United States, with the Iran-Iraq war serving as an economic weapon against these countries.

Quite logically, then, the government began printing paper money, increasing the amount of money in circulation to staggering proportions. The sale of our gold reserves, the increased oil production, and the arms purchases were the most visible signs that the war was going to continue. As arms purchases climbed to $40 billion, the first signs of the war spreading to the Persian Gulf appeared. The Americans threatened to send their forces to the region and six adjacent countries decided to form an alliance.

The theories of the Israeli Right were winning converts. According to them, the Middle East is a region without states that has always been nothing but a mosaic of communities grouped into empires. A return to its original state was therefore necessary, and who better than Israel to play the role of federator? Only war could make this dream a reality. In addition, by promoting a war in the Gulf, the proponents of this theory alleviated the pressure on the Israeli borders and made the Iran-Iraq war the number one problem in the Middle East. The center of gravity of all the region's conflicts was thus shifted from Israel to the Persian Gulf.

The first cracks in the facade of denial date from this same period, with the trip to Egypt of an Iraqi delegation. For the Baghdad regime, it was a matter of survival, the Egyptians forgetting for the moment that they had been excluded from the Arab League at Iraq's initiative. This rapprochement with Egypt—a very populous country and a supplier of labor—was another clear indication that the war would continue.

•

The decline in oil prices, the drop in economic activity and its corollary, lower incomes, caused a mass rural exodus in Iran. The gap between household income and expenditures widened. With the mint operating at top capacity, inflation raged and in its wake brought poverty. Rationing was introduced and the working class fell under state economic control, which, together with the rural exodus, enabled the regime very quickly to involve a growing number of rural youth in the war.

Because of this sociological upheaval, the regime was able to consider dispensing with the army. The glorification of martyrdom among young people of humble origins was easy. This period is therefore characterized by contempt for the economy and a rise in fascism: exploit poverty to glorify victory.

THE MULLAHS DELAY THE OFFENSIVE

Even before I left, it was obvious that our army could drive the Iraqis back across the border in four months, as we had planned. It took a year to achieve this objective, however, because the mullahs wanted neither an end to the war nor a rapid succession of victories. Closely timed, successful offensives would have demonstrated the strength of the army, which it would then have been extremely difficult to replace with the Guards.

Four operations were needed to end the Iraqi occupation of Iranian territory. The first was executed in October 1981 in the south, in Abadan, a town famous for its oil refineries. The Iraqi forces that had crossed the Caroun River were cut off from the rear and isolated by a blockade. The second was staged two months later, in December. Although it was a minor offensive at the center of the front, it nevertheless enabled our forces to reach the border, and if the mullahs had wanted them to, our troops could have advanced into Iraqi territory. The third attack, in the Desfoul region, did not take place until March 1982. This operation, completely successful, led to the capture of a great many Iraqi prisoners.

It nevertheless took them nine months to liberate 15 percent of the territory, whereas we had recovered 50 percent in just one month. This success was the more surprising since the best

•

technicians, strategists, and senior officers were gone, having been exiled, executed, or assassinated.

After this victory, Rafsanjani, in a Friday prayer meeting, had the audacity to say, "All of this could have been accomplished a year ago; it was Bani-Sadr who delayed everything." Thus, he admitted publicly that these plans existed before. Another three months were to pass before the great Khorramshahr offensive drove the Iraqis back across the border. On June 21, 1982, the Iraqis officially announced the withdrawal of their forces to the international border, which they had already offered to do several times before, most notably in May 1981.

I thought, despite everything, that the mullahs would continue the war. I said this in an interview with Pierre Salinger on ABC, the American television network, adding that they would continue until they were defeated. At this specific moment, they had three choices: a war of attrition on the border, a war on Iraqi territory, or the cessation of hostilities.

The third option was the least probable because, politically, it implied a period of explanations within the regime. Two questions would arise immediately: why was this military plan, which Bani-Sadr had described as achievable in May 1981, postponed for a year? Many lives would have been spared and a great deal of money saved. Why, if they wanted to end the war politically, did they not do it in June 1981 when the four ministers from the nonaligned countries and the leaders of the Islamic Conference urged us to do so? No explanation would be possible with a victorious and, therefore, dangerous army.

A war of attrition within the borders could not be justified, at least not at first.

I therefore announced that they would choose to launch attacks on Iraqi territory. This option implied an ideological shift. Until then, it was solely a question of defending the country against aggression. Suddenly, the objective was "Jerusalem by way of Karbala," the holy city of Shiism in Iraq. This new decision would necessitate purges and the replacement of the army by the Guards.

The maktabis' key position was now official and recognized by all. With my removal from office and condemnation for refusing to submit to the Imam, the principle of obedience replaced the principle of democracy. In July 1982, the entire country was required to obey Khomeini. The word *freedom* no longer had any application in Iran. Khomeini himself explained, "We gave the political parties freedom. They betrayed us by using it against the revolution; this is why we have put an end to their freedom." He added, "Freedom exists, except the freedom to oppose Islam." The Shah said that all freedoms were enjoyed in Iran except the freedom to commit treason. A popular joke in those days was that the freedom to commit treason was the exclusive privilege of the Shah, who did not want anyone competing with him in an area in which he excelled.

Violence became the regime's chief tool: in the war, in the repression of opponents, in the government, and in the management of businesses. The "Hezbollah method," as they said, meant getting results by force and immediately.

This, then, is how the mullahs—ideologically, politically, economically, and militarily—prepared for perpetual war.

After the Khorramshahr victory, Khomeini began talking about an "Islamic belt in the Middle East," a group of Shiite countries under his heel that would include Iran, Iraq, Syria, and Lebanon. In this same period, the concept of Bonapartism was again bandied about, but I was no longer there. Whom did they fear, then, if not the army? Strangely, they had not allowed the army to continue its advance into Iraqi territory through Mandali, at the center of the front. This breach, located 120 kilometers from Baghdad, would have made it possible to cut the country in two at minimum cost. They chose to attack in the south, in Basra, which Khomeini wanted to take because Rafsanjani had put it into his head that the fall of this city would lead to the downfall of Saddam Hussein. We all knew that this was untrue, because a study conducted by the military had concluded that an attack in the south would be a lengthy, suicidal operation with no strategic value. Basra was a ghost town, an empty port, of no use to the enemy since we had total control of the sea. They launched this attack to prolong the war indefinitely and, as usual, to prevent a decisive victory by the army. In all dictatorships, the army is both the backbone and the rival of the regime; defeated or victorious, it is dangerous. This was the case with the Shah, who, during the revolution—and I have the documents to prove it—was more

•

179

afraid of his army than of the people, to such an extent that he was reluctant to call out the army for fear of being overthrown by it.

The Guards had not yet become a force capable of competing with the army. A victorious army could have deposed the mullahs, suppressed the Islamic revolutionary organizations and institutions, and seized power. I felt no such fear myself, for if the regime had remained democratic, a victorious army, having become a national army because of the revolution, would no longer be a threat.

New slogans heralded the mullahs' "human wave" tactic, which was to cause so many deaths. Shamekhani, who was the commander of the Guards and is now the commander of naval forces, said, "Unlike Bani-Sadr who cried 'tank versus tank'; we say 'bodies versus tanks.'" They also sent children only fourteen and fifteen years of age to Basra. The other slogan of the day was equally revealing: "No tactics, no technology." We were entering the era of military irrationality, which was to continue until 1985. Khomeini was well aware that an attack within Iraqi territory, if not quick and decisive, would result in the consolidation of the regime of Saddam Hussein.

The foreign powers did not do anything to end the war either. Had the army been properly equipped, it could have entered Baghdad in eight days, which is what everyone wanted to avoid at all costs. The Soviets wanted the hostilities to continue, counting on the parties they secretly supported in Iran to infiltrate the regime. Also, the Iran-Iraq war deflected media attention from their problem in Afghanistan. The Americans were more desirous than ever of regaining control of Iran. They had incited the war for this very reason and it could not end before they got what they wanted. The politics of oil linked the two governments, despite the apparent conflicts. Reagan, Khomeini, the same struggle— this slogan became more apt than ever when Irangate broke out. The war was bound to continue for one final reason. In a country with a population of 40 million, what would become of the 65 percent of young people under twenty-five years of age who had no past and no present and who based all their hopes on the future? Leaving them to their fate was out of the question since they might well become a destructive force. It was therefore necessary to channel this youthful energy into the war and the export of crisis in the world—through terrorism, if necessary. There is no other solution for a regime that has deprived the people of all economic and cultural prospects. Beheshti may be dead, but his vision survives: the mullahs take control of the state and replace the old institutions. The only possible outcome was the disappearance of the regular army, the final step in the process. Since the Revolutionary Guards could not replace an army so recently and so repeatedly successful, continuation of the war was essential.

18

1982–85

Khomeini Pulls the Strings

FROM THE INTERNAL, EXTERNAL, AND MILITARY VIEWPOINTS, the 1982-84 period is characterized by major upheavals. Everything was jumbled together, and then, gradually, as in a flour mill, the different elements were separated. Intoxicated by successes on the front, the mullahs had only one battle cry: "Down with the Saddam Hussein regime!" Not for a second did they imagine that their actions were strengthening rather than weakening the Iraqi Baath Party, or that they were promoting an alliance between the Iraqi Sunnis and Shiites instead of pitting them against each other. It seemed obvious that the Shiites, afraid of being labeled "anti-Arab," would join forces with the Sunnis. For Rafsanjani, Saddam Hussein's removal was not enough; a military victory was essential. The mullahs actually hoped to eliminate both armies: the Iraqi army, in order to establish a Khomeini-style regime in Iraq, and ours, in order to replace it with the Revolutionary Guards. They purposely fanned anti-Iraqi sentiment by proclaiming that "the Arabs are Iran's biggest enemy." An article by William H. Sullivan, the last U.S. ambassador to Iran, encouraged them in their all-out strategy. Sullivan recognized the weakness of the Iraqi regime and predicted its downfall, but this is not what made the biggest impression on Khomeini; it was the end of the article, written in the form of a historical fiction, in which Sullivan described the aftermath of an Iranian victory. He envisioned nothing more or less than an alliance between Syria, southern Lebanon, Iraq, and Iran to menace Israel. Tehran would thus become the leader of a Shiite bloc, against which a Sunni bloc would inevitably form. This idea of a Shiite belt, which had already taken root in Khomeini's mind, was not totally without precedent since the Shah, despite his anti-Islamic policy, represented himself as the protector of the world's Shiites. This thesis of Sullivan's was extremely gratifying to Khomeini, who circulated it among the officials of his regime.

Khomeini stated publicly that the economic and human price of victory had to be paid. This new policy explains the considerable loss of life at that time.

In the beginning, our air force completely dominated the airspace. The situation was completely reversed in 1984. By then, we had only fifty F-4 Phantom and ten F-14 Tomcat aircraft left. Our casualties had increased tenfold and the numbers were horrifying: 300,000; 400,000; 500,000 dead. Not long ago, the regime published statistics indicating a total of 123,230 deaths for the entire war. Montazeri disputed this figure, considering it an insult to the people since we lost nearly one million men and women in the war. With the regime persisting in its "bodies versus tanks" tactic and continuing to send waves of children aged thirteen and fourteen years in front of Iraqi machine guns to break the lines of defense, the first signs of weariness were not long in coming, especially among adult soldiers, who began wondering why they were fighting the war. Khomeini and his advisers immediately took stock of the situation and acted accordingly. The law on military service was amended, and harsh penalties were instituted for anyone attempting to avoid recruitment. When the war no longer had anything to do with defending the country, many Iranians balked at being sent to the front. A black market trade in military exemption papers sprang up and a mass exodus of young people fleeing compulsory enlistment began.

With the war as the sole focus of the political, cultural, and even the economic aspects of society, young people in Iran had only two futures to look forward to: government employment or enlistment. Under the Shah there were 1.2 million government employees. Although we reduced the number to 1.1 million in the early years of the revolution, in 1985 there were nearly two million government employees. If a government career failed to interest them, young people had no other choice but to enlist in the Basij and end up on the front. In 1985, a number of high school students refused to take their final exams to avoid the choice of having to leave the country or being made martyrs by Iraqi bullets. However, it would be untrue to say that four years after the start of the war the people refused to go into combat. These were merely signs that were appearing.

In this period, major attacks were spaced about six months apart. Each time, the enemy lines were broken by wave upon wave of soldiers, but the lack of logistics prevented our army from consolidating its position so completely, in fact, that almost every offensive turned into a disaster. Iraq, in response to these waves and to break the morale of the people, stepped up its attacks on the cities. It was a very painful moment in the war, observed in January 1983 by the UN experts sent to Iran at the government's request. This visit itself marked a change in the leaders' attitude toward the United Nations, even though it only involved the submission of a report.

In 1983, the war on the cities intensified, with missiles punctuating the usual aerial bombing. The attack of February 1983, which ended in a resounding failure, marked a new twist in the mullahs' strategy. It coincided with the U.S. announcement that the war had lessened in intensity and the acceptance of an Algerian fact-finding mission by the Iranian government. On returning home, the Algerian foreign affairs minister announced that Iran no longer insisted on the removal of Saddam Hussein before entering into negotiations. The mullahs denied this for the sake of appearances, but it was indeed a complete about-face. Insiders noted two currents stirring within the regime: one in favor of political reconciliation and the other characterized by international terrorism, export of the revolution, and perpetual war. Khomeini constantly made use of these two currents to ensure his own preeminence.

In this period, the latter faction was in the ascendant, especially since Khomeini, enthralled by the idea of a Shiite belt,

•

was leaning in the same direction. The Revolutionary Guards, believing themselves protected, took more and more liberties with the law. Despite the intervention of Khamenei, president of the Republic, the Guards forcibly recruited some of the country's six million unemployed. Their numbers rose very quickly from 30,000 to more than 300,000, with all the problems that such growth entails, even in the regular army.

IRAQI DIPLOMATIC SUCCESSES

The Iraqi regime's first political reaction to these staggering attacks by waves of human beings was Saddam Hussein's announcement that he would request support from the United States if necessary. Until then, public opinion in the Arab world was opposed to the American presence, but this obstacle was quietly removed. During this same period, Saddam Hussein received aid from Egypt, which sent pilots and workers to Iraq.

This fear of Iran manifested itself in the formation of the Organization for Gulf State Cooperation, which made two important decisions: the creation of a joint air force and the construction of a pipeline to offset the consequences of a possible closing of the Gulf. Two axes were formed: Tehran-Tel Aviv and Riyadh-Cairo-Baghdad. Only the Tehran-Tel Aviv axis was hostile, but each turned to the United States for aid to continue fighting the other.

Iraq was scoring points on the international scene. The Conference of Arab States, which had accepted the return of Egypt, officially gave its support. In January 1984, the Islamic Conference of Casablanca also approved the return of Egypt and organized a reconciliation mission, thus confirming Iraq's desire to end to the war. Headed by Mustafa Liaz, Senegal's foreign affairs minister, the representatives of the Islamic countries came to Iran to propose a ceasefire, the observance of the Algiers Agreements, the creation of a reparations fund, and an investigative commission to determine the aggressor. The mullahs refused this offer, which had been accepted by Iraq. Iran's international isolation became even more pronounced when the United Nations Assembly, by 119 votes and 5 abstentions, condemned the war and demanded peace.

•

During this same period, the Khomeini regime sent troops to Lebanon, ostensibly to fight Israel but in reality to organize international terrorism with Lebanese integrationists.

On October 21, 1984, Moshe Arens, Israeli ambassador to the United States, admitted that his country was selling American arms to Iran. This admission, together with Israel's invasion of Lebanon and the Israeli right-wing theories about the disappearance of four states in the region (Syria, Lebanon, Jordan, and Iraq), created a feeling of unease in Iran, where this information was widely disseminated. Even within the regime, a current of protest surfaced, which both the Right and the Left naturally tried to turn to account.

The Right triumphed, taking its bearings from the rejection of Israeli right-wing theories by the Americans and the momentary weakness of Soviet policy in the region, which resulted from the Soviet Union's entanglement in Afghanistan and its frustration in Lebanon and in the nationalist movements it supported. The Right maneuvered so cleverly that it was able to present rapprochement with the United States as the only possible solution.

During this period of political uncertainty, Khomeini, to create the appearance of stability, asked the people to elect a new constituent assembly of eighty mullahs, called "experts," to choose his successor. He wanted to show the entire world that Iran is the most stable country since the Guide's successor is chosen while the Guide is still living. Neither the Soviet Union nor the Catholic church had ever done anything like this. Of the 150,000 mullahs the clerics claim are in Iran, only 147 named a candidate. It was a failure, but a few months later these eighty mullahs nevertheless appointed Montazeri as Khomeini's successor, his name to remain a secret until the Imam's death.

In 1984, in Qom, the Left/Right split between the mullahs became official. Pamphlets signed "The Vigilant Clerics" were distributed at night, attacking the ossified, unrealistic, right-wing clerics, supporters of unrestrained liberalism. This split also manifested itself implicitly within the regime. Prior to this, the Right never dared to express political and religious support for private property and economic liberalism. This division, increasingly acute in the highest circles, was as yet invisible to outsiders. It was not until the second parliamentary elections, in

April 1984, that the factions came out into the open. These elections also revealed just how wide the gulf was between the people and their leaders. No more than 10 percent of the electorate voted. Bazargan's party, refusing to support the mullahs, declined to nominate any candidates.

Khamenei, again elected president, wanted someone other than Mousavi—reputedly a leftist—to be prime minister. Despite Khomeini's refusal, nearly all of the deputies on the Right voted against the Musavi government, enabling the Left to accuse them of being hostile to the line of the Imam.

A NEW RAPPROCHEMENT WITH THE AMERICANS

After the first instance of cooperation between the United States and Iran in connection with the Soviet spy recruited by the Americans—which made it possible to dismantle the KGB networks in the region—gestures of sympathy and goodwill between the two nations became increasingly frequent.

In October 1984, we published information that has never been refuted concerning a secret meeting between Velayati, the Iranian foreign affairs minister, and George Shultz, Reagan's secretary of state. Surprisingly, at a time when the Americans were reinforcing their strike force in the region, an official in the Khomeini regime bluntly stated that Iran was still the Americans' bulwark against communism.

Then the revelations about American arms sales began proliferating. Dr. Yazdi, Bazargan's foreign affairs minister, revealed that the United States, via Spain, had sold Iran $3 billion worth of arms. During this period, in 1984, Khomeini suddenly began talking about an imminent victory, although the military situation warranted no such optimism. He based this optimism on the new rapprochement with the Americans, which, a short time later, did permit a few minor victories such as Majnoun and Fao. The Americans began talking about changes in the Iranian regime and the appearance of a moderate trend. Rafsanjani's name began to circulate as the United States' man.

At the same time, Khomeini used the regime's extremist wing to maintain a hold on the international terrorist movement developing in Lebanon, as evidenced by the blowing up of the U.S. embassy in Beirut and of the French forces' headquarters. Medhi Hashemi, one of the organizers of the bombings, enjoyed growing influence, especially since he was the protégé of Montazeri, recently appointed as the Imam's official successor.

The regime's left wing benefited from the abortive attacks on the front, the falling oil prices, and the mullahs' statements accusing the Americans of fraud. Relations with the United States were uneven. In the Reagan administration, there were two opposing camps. One wanted to attack Iran and the other to pursue the course initiated with the 1980 agreement. In the end, the latter option was chosen. Sadeh Tabatabai revealed that in July 1984, Hans-Dietrich Genscher, the German foreign affairs minister, had served as "Mr. Fix-It" by traveling to Iran ostensibly to negotiate business contracts but in reality to repair the frayed threads of the dialogue with the Americans. To thwart this mission, the regime's hard-liners organized the hijacking of an Air France jet to Tehran on July 31. Their plan failed, however, because the hijackers quickly released their hostages, too soon to prevent the Right's reconciliation with the Americans.

The first visible signs that totalitarianism was faltering appeared in 1983. The butchery resulting from the continuing use of the human wave tactic, despite the recovery of all our territory, encouraged popular resistance to the regime. In January 1983, Khomeini himself gave the signal for this change of direction. He drafted an eight-point manifesto criticizing the judiciary and the abuses of the Guards, acknowledging that the people had rights and that the Guide was not all-powerful. He went on to say that the idea of an inquisition is contrary to Islam and that the forces of law and order must not invade people's homes without good reason. This was the modest beginning of a reversal that continues to this day. The Right took advantage of this turnaround to take over the economic sector, particularly by seizing several key positions. They even managed to prevent the publication of a book by a highly respected cleric, Motahari, who was assassinated at the beginning of the revolution, on the pretext that it was about economic justice and the adaptation of capitalism to Islam.

Left/Right disputes were now focused on the economy: liberalism or state control? The conflict became increasingly bitter

•

as the country's economic situation worsened. At the beginning of this period, OPEC production was already too high, which made the oil market uncontrollable. On February 19 and 20, 1983, the British and the Norwegians lowered their prices by $3.50 and $5.50 a barrel, and in late March 1984, OPEC agreed to a 15 percent price cut. We were experiencing a reverse oil crisis; this meant a loss of power for OPEC and a victory for the West, which was taking its revenge for the previous crises. In the Iranian economy, the repercussions appeared in the form of higher inflation, a 100 percent increase in free market prices, a drop in national production, higher unemployment, and an enormous budget deficit.

In 1980, the Iranian government spent $20 billion and earned $14 billion. Two years after the coup d'état, in 1983, expenses totaled $33 billion and revenues $10 billion. This trend continues today, with the government preparing a budget geared primarily toward defense and running the bureaucracy, while production continues to decline.

This inflationary trend encouraged large-scale speculation in four types of products: gold (especially old coins), carpets, antiques, and—since Tehran had not yet been bombed—construction. In June 1984, in a speech before the deputies, Khomeini acknowledged the country's difficulties for the first time, especially the economic paralysis, the high cost of living, the insecurity, and the lack of freedom. The total debt up to that date was $60 billion. Iran became a country without a budget and found it increasingly difficult to sell its oil in a depressed market.

At the close of this period, despite the economic crisis and the people's growing hostility to the war, there was no sign that Khomeini wanted to end it. He hoped for a victory, but mature reflection made it obvious that it would put the country in an impossible situation. Suppose that Saddam Hussein were overthrown and Iran established a new regime in Iraq. An army would have to be organized. What would its composition be? Would the old structure and personnel be retained? Would an Iraqi Shiite army be formed or would the Iranian army establish itself in Iraq? Iran lacked the resources to maintain occupation forces and it would have been impossible to create a Shiite army or to retain the old army without taking enormous risks.

•

In every case, Khomeini was the loser. He would also lose if he settled for a war of attrition on the border, because Saddam Hussein could request arms and money from other wealthy Arab nations and Khomeini did not have this option. Moreover, a lengthy war of attrition would necessitate competition in the sale of oil, causing an even greater drop in prices.

The mullahs therefore had nothing to gain by prolonging the war; unfortunately, the internal conflicts and the totalitarian regime's lack of cohesiveness made it essential that the war continue. Even if he had wanted to, Khomeini would have found it extremely difficult to end the hostilities, because the dominant faction at the time wanted to continue the war on Iraqi territory. The Guards had infiltrated all of the regime's vital institutions. They had suppressed economic liberalism and had obtained a monopoly on foreign trade and arms purchases. The minister of the Bazaar had been replaced by one of their men.

The Left, temporarily in the ascendant, applauded the Imam's use of terrorism to blackmail the United States. The Right, however, was not laying down its weapons; it was simply biding its time. Rafsanjani had even tried to establish contacts with the regime's opponents in Europe, some of whom were ready to listen to him.

A DIFFICULT COEXISTENCE

Not I, though. I followed these events very closely, and I knew that the regime was in a bad way. Throughout this period, my alliance with Rajavi survived. Our first clashes had occurred as soon as we arrived in France. The first thing Rajavi did was to replace our agreement with a plan to put him in total control of our resistance movement, which at the time consisted of my supporters and some organizations that had supported him as a presidential candidate in the first election. Naturally, I refused to let him take over. He could do what he wanted with the others, but I was not about to answer for him. He concurred and wrote me a letter that preserved my independence vis-à-vis the council he was going to form.

We quickly differed on another principle as well: freedom.

•

Being a true Stalinist, he did not believe in it. My argument was that despotism cannot be fought with a despotic ideology, totalitarianism against totalitarianism. The only alternative for me was the organization of a force that would defend the original principles of the revolution, thus avoiding a repetition of the Algerian experience.

I soon realized that Rajavi, who was not well liked in Iran, wanted to use my popularity to attract to his organization as many of the regime's opponents as possible. After a few months, the language of the Mujahedeen became ambiguous. They began talking about hegemony, democracy, and independence in extremely vague terms. The solution proposed by Gassemlou intrigued Rajavi. It consisted of negotiating with the superpowers and Iran's enemies to obtain the resources necessary to overthrow Khomeini. I wrote a manifesto based on the experience of our revolution and on a historical analysis of revolutionary movements in general. I said that when an ideology responds to the basic needs of a society, especially to end an identity crisis, that society begins to move; that this movement will be successful if all the factions espouse a single ideology; and that any group seeking to take control of the movement must obtain outside assistance. In the contemporary history of Iran, despotic movements relying on force—royalist, clerical, and left-wing totalitarian—have been on the wane for a hundred years. There is nothing to suggest that this trend will cease. The monarchy, which was the symbol of this type of social organization, has disappeared and now the people are intensifying their resistance to the new clerical totalitarianism.

In an article, Rajavi penned a slogan about the Guards: "Kill them wherever you find them." I disagreed because the Guards are mercenaries and civil servants. Why blame them? It is the regime that must be destroyed, not them. Fairly quickly, Rajavi suggested sparing the Americans and the Iraqis in our propaganda, despite the fact that we had left Iran to denounce not only the regime but also the responsibility of these two countries in the war.

On January 8, 1983, Paul Vieille, a sociologist friend of mine, asked me, at the recommendation of Edgard Pisani, if I was ready to meet with Tarek Aziz, the Iraqi foreign affairs minister. I

•

refused on principle and because I had no control over what he might say after the meeting. The same day, Rajavi came to tell me that one of our Palestinian intermediaries also proposed a meeting with this same individual. I said that we could agree to his presence in Auvers-sur-Oise only if he came as the envoy of a defeated regime and acknowledged us as the representatives of a victimized but victorious nation. Rajavi decided to meet with him on this condition. I added that he need not be granted a very long interview.

At 10:00 the next morning I opened my shutters and saw Tarek Aziz's car parked in the courtyard. It remained there until 5:00 in the evening. You can imagine what a state I was in. I understood it all. Rajavi came to report on their conversation and to read a joint statement they had prepared. I could not believe my ears. It was a pact, the main objective of which was to overthrow Khomeini. There was nothing I could do about it, except to give interviews to express my opposition. The rupture was complete, and yet I did not regret attempting to ally myself with Rajavi because I had hoped, through this alliance, to promote the growth of his organization. It was essential that the resistance be founded on the principles of the revolution and Rajavi had signed an agreement to that effect. By joining forces with Rajavi and his supporters, I had wanted to prevent us—after suffering through royalist and then clerical totalitarianism—from falling into leftist totalitarianism. Although Rajavi's organization was small, the danger existed. Look at Khomeini. At first, he represented only himself; it was the Shah's regime that magnified his importance. The mullahs did everything they could to increase the importance of these small organizations.

I failed; it was impossible to lead them toward democracy. Still, it was worth the effort.

The final break came a year later. In the meantime, our National Resistance Council had approved a peace plan based on the 1975 Algiers Agreement, the formation of a committee to monitor the ceasefire, the exchange of prisoners, reparations, the return of refugees expelled by Iraq before the war, amnesty, and negotiations for a lasting peace based on national sovereignty and the independence of both countries. When this text was published in the newspapers, the Iraqi information minister

•

announced his country's assent. Thus, for the third time, Iraq agreed to a peace plan based on the 1975 agreements.

Sensing that a rapprochement was near between part of the Resistance Council and the Iraqis—and, therefore, the Americans— I thought that it was time to publish documents proving the existence of the ties between Khomeini and Reagan. Up to that point, we had given explanations but had produced no evidence.

In March 1984, therefore, *Le Canard enchaîné* published documents concerning the Israeli arms purchases of March 1981. The Council also approved a plan for Kurdish autonomy. Gassemlou's initial plan had basically called for partition, but I objected and threatened to resign, and since their agreement with Iraq was not yet sealed, they needed me and were forced to yield.

In the following months, our alliance deteriorated. Rajavi tried in vain to attract Iranian youths who were disillusioned with the mullahs' regime but who were wary of his totalitarian tendencies. Consequently, Rajavi drew closer to the Iraqis, who of course offered to provide him with financial support and to pay the living expenses of the refugees in France.

In March 1984, the newspaper *Enghelab Eslami* published an article entitled "The Lies of Tarek Aziz." Rajavi pounced on it and every evening for three months tried to convince me that we should go to Iraq, settle near the border, and appeal to the Iranians to join in a march to Tehran to overthrow the regime. I thought that this plan was crazy, and I told Rajavi every day that his idea was pure madness. As a result of this article, he wrote a fourteen-page letter to explain that I was stabbing him in the back and to announce our separation.

I returned to my apartment in Cachan and organized my own group. Intermediaries tried to reconcile us, but I could not get him the things he so desperately wanted: arms and money, which the Iraqis were only too glad to provide. He imagined that in the long run, this alliance, born of necessity, would be forgotten. Fortunately, the Iranian people have forgotten nothing, and now Rajavi, a pawn in the settlement of the Iran-Iraq conflict, is discredited forever.

I then based my personal strategy on the establishment of a continuing dialogue with the Iranian people through press releases, cassette tapes, and articles, which I have secretly circulated in Iran. In exile, I wanted to condemn the arms sales and the role of the United States. In July 1984, following Genscher's trip to Iran, I denounced the initial contacts preparing the way for the new era of U.S.-Iranian cooperation, which would later become Irangate. My sources in Iran did—and still do—supply me with stacks of information, which I study very closely in order to analyze the day-to-day evolution of the regime and of Iranian society.

I also wanted to prove that by remaining independent, by living in exile without funds, it is nevertheless possible to retain political credibility and not be forgotten by the people.

19

THE REGIME VACILLATES

IN THE YEARS SINCE 1985, THE POLITICAL LANDSCAPE—
somewhat static at first—has changed. Between the Right,
represented by Khamenei, and Montazeri's leftist group, which is
growing like a cancer, a third, center-left group has formed. Its
proponents include Rafsanjani and Mousavi, the prime minister,
as well as some of the Revolutionary Guards and part of
parliament.

Ideological and political warfare has erupted among these
groups in six religious centers: Qom, Mashhad, Isfahan, Tabriz,
Shiraz, and Hamadan. All of these cities have strategic importance
on the geopolitical map of Iran.

In 1985, clerical opposition was on the rise. More and more
mullahs were distancing themselves from the regime. Golpahegani,
for example, publicly expressed dissent by proclaiming that I was
a good president.

Many young people wanted to study Islam from a different
perspective, to rediscover the original logic of the revolution.
Rafsanjani began to say that Bani-Sadr's thinking was good, but
not the man himself.

Politically, the top level of the regime was being torn apart;

cracks were visible everywhere, even—and especially—within the Islamic Republic Party. Rafsanjani, addressing a seminar for the commanders of the armed forces on January 9, 1985, admitted that there were three factions within his party: the Left, which did not believe in private property; the Right; and his, which cooperated with the other two. In March 1985, a seemingly forgotten concept was resurrected by Montazeri when he spoke of a creeping coup d'état perpetrated by Rafsanjani.

During this period, my newspaper, *Enghelab Eslami*, which is published in Paris, printed an analysis of the regime, which created a great stir in Iran. I listed three criteria for measuring the stability of a regime: a majority must believe that the regime is the best one possible, its leaders must be competent, and they must chose the right means and objectives in the problem sectors, which, in our case, meant oil, the war, foreign policy, and exporting revolution. With none of these conditions for the minimum stability of the regime being fulfilled, I predicted its eventual collapse. This analysis is still being discussed in Iran today. This general warfare among the governing authorities was manifested in overt acts. Organizations created by the regime were attacked. The leftist newspaper *Sobhe Adadegan*, for example, has been banned since September 1985.

Conflicts also raged among the mullahs. They forbade each other to publish religious works. It is important to realize, in this regard, that each doctor of theology is free to publish his own opinions and recommendations and that each Shiite chooses to follow whatever teaching he prefers. Obviously, the centralistic, authoritarian sovereignty of the Islamic jurist is incompatible with this religious structure, which permits freedom of expression.

The year 1985 is significant because of the presidential elections. The candidacy of Bazargan, the prime minister appointed by Khomeini at the beginning of the revolution, was rejected by the Council of Guardians of the Constitution on the grounds of incompetence; Khamenei was therefore returned to the presidency more or less by default. Khamenei supposedly was not interested in running again, but the Imam, in his desire to keep the various factions in check, forced him to. After his reelection, Khamenei announced in a speech in Mashhad that he wanted to reorganize the government because it had not done a

•

good job. The race was on for the position of prime minister. Each group tried to shove its candidate into the spotlight. To publicize its favorite, for example, the Right fabricated an interview by Jean Gueyras, a French journalist on the staff of *Le Monde*, with Azari Ghoumi, a clergyman from Qom and editor of the right-wing newspaper *Ressalat*. In this interview, every word of which was false, Ghoumi described at length the statesmanlike qualities of Madavi-Khani, his candidate. I condemned this tactic in an article, which hit parliament like a bomb.

This race for the nomination was entirely futile since Khomeini, as usual, beat everyone to the punch by reinstalling the previous government. This did not prevent ninety-nine deputies from voting in parliament against the Mousavi government. According to his aides, this act of insubordination upset Khomeini, who was beginning to sense the limits of his charisma, even within the regime. In my time, it might have been said that I was preaching another Islam and that my opposition to the Imam was logical, but what could be said about these deputies, all of whom were maktabis? Everyone realized that the era of blind allegiance to Khomeini had come to an end.

With a right-wing president and a left-wing government, each trying to make the most of its position, a new wave of purges began. Anyone with even a scrap of power began hunting opponents.

It was in this period that Montazeri's appointment as the Imam's successor, which was supposed to remain a secret, was revealed by a religious leader in Ghazvin, thus setting off a powderkeg. The quarrel assumed such proportions that Montazeri was forced to send a letter to the Assembly stating that he was prepared to renounce the appointment and that someone else would have to be chosen. The purpose of this extremely humble attitude was to calm things down. Opinion was divided on this paradoxical appointment; certain individuals thought that Montazeri had been chosen merely for the use that could be made of him, a time-honored tactic of proven effectiveness in politics.

In October 1986, the religious stronghold of Qom fell under right-wing control, isolating Montazeri. Khomeini, the expert strategist, chose this moment to attack the Right in preparation for a sudden, violent attack on Hashemi's leftist group.

•

Events then accelerated. In late October, Medhi Hashemi, his brother Hadi Hashemi, Montazeri's son-in-law, and several members of their circle were arrested.

IRANGATE EXPOSED

On November 3, *Al Shiraa*, an Arabic newspaper in Beirut, revealed that Robert McFarlane had visited Tehran. On the fourth, Rafsanjani acknowledged the facts, explaining that the Americans had been carrying false passports.

It took five months for this visit to become known, since it took place on May 27. Apparently, on that date, the Hashemi group had tried to organize a demonstration in front of the Independence Hotel where the Americans were staying, the purpose being to counter the Right's attempted rapprochement with the United States. Rafsanjani intervened personally to stop them. Throughout this period, conflicts were smoldering within the regime. Everyone knew it, but it took the arrest of Hashemi for the whole story to come out through Hafez el Assad and the Beirut newspaper. For myself, I was aware that a trip to Iran had been made, but I did not know who was involved.

After the arrest of the Hashemi group, the situation worsened. At the top of the hierarchy, the Right had just taken control of the religious centers, and Khomeini went into action at the grass roots to restrain impatient youths anxious to do away with all of the system's old clans. Dropped by the people and the country's six major religious centers, deprived of his faithful Hashemi, Montazeri was drastically isolated.

Political change accelerated more than anyone outside the country could have imagined, leading in June 1987 to the dissolution of the Islamic Republic Party, the backbone of the regime for seven years.

After Irangate was exposed, Khomeini, willingly or not, took two contradictory steps. First, he strengthened his absolute supremacy as Guide; then, he set about destroying the ideological and political bases of this supremacy one by one.

Khomeini increased his power by forming a tribunal to judge clerics he believed were corrupt; he secretly reinstituted the

Revolutionary Council, which still enjoys a shadowy existence today; and he proclaimed his own absolute supremacy over parliament and the Council of Guardians of the Constitution. But he then decided to give political interest absolute priority over religious law, thereby destroying the religious power structure he had so carefully erected. In August 1987, he announced that a council to identify political interests would soon be formed, consisting of a few carefully chosen clerics who would decide, on a case-by-case basis, how Koranic law should be applied. These clerics could therefore arbitrarily authorize the enforcement of a measure contrary to Islamic law, without anyone being able to say anything about it. This council would be responsible for settling disputes between parliament and the Council of Guardians of the Constitution.

This day-to-day tactic for keeping the ship afloat did not have the expected results. In September 1987, Khomeini had to acknowledge publicly that the country was going astray. Montazeri, jumping at the chance to outdo Khomeini, talked about shipwreck and attacked the Right.

In November 1987, Khomeini suddenly changed his will. No one knew what he changed, but there were many suppositions. He was then faced with a terrible dilemma: should he eliminate Rafsanjani, as a powerful faction in the regime demanded? Seven deputies even submitted a written question to the government on this subject. Or should he give Rafsanjani full authority to pursue his policies? Apparently, he chose the latter course, but without saying so, in order to leave some room for maneuvering with the Left. Surprisingly, in April 1988, as parliament was being reelected, Khomeini intervened to remove most of the ninety-nine right-wing deputies, sparing a few for appearance's sake.

The end of 1987 found the regime divided, disoriented, in turmoil from top to bottom. Montazeri, still the Imam's official successor, adapted his views to the circumstances in order to survive in this quagmire. He became an impassioned advocate of freedom and acted the part of Cassandra by listing the regime's fifteen economic, social, cultural, and political dilemmas. Rafsanjani was still trying to get rid of Mousavi, who, without power over his ministers, submitted his resignation several times, only to have it rejected by Khomeini, as expected. The Revolutionary Guards published portraits of Rafsanjani with the American flag as a background.

Certain officials wanted me to return, because they saw it as a way out for themselves. Bazargan, the only opponent who was tolerated, added a new twist to the general collapse by threatening to destroy his own organization to protest the role of "fall guy" he was forced to play.

THE OPPOSITION DISCREDITED

Among opponents of the regime living abroad, the status of the monarchists and the Mujahedeen has changed. The monarchists have been losing ground ever since September 1985, when everyone realized that the Americans were no longer interested in reestablishing a royalist regime in Iran. The final blow was administered by Irangate, which revealed not only that the CIA was paying the monarchists but that the monarchists were working with the mullahs in the arms deals. They lost considerable credibility with their own supporters and are now reduced to vainly begging for support in the Arab countries.

Rajavi's position is no better. He soon had to explain that his organization, created specifically to continue the struggle against the United States, had become an information agency for the CIA. As Richard W. Murphy told it, the Mujahedeen nearly rivaled Israel as far as the quality of information was concerned. Rajavi justified this change by explaining that revolution is the culminating point of morality—in other words, the end justifies the means. This is the morality of totalitarianism. To justify his actions, Rajavi published a paper on the ideological transformation guiding his behavior. He had the members of his organization ratify it in order to keep them in his power. The Mujahedeen have become a sort of sect, wholly devoted to their leader and without influence in Iran, especially since their fighting alongside the Iraqis discredited them forever. Before the ceasefire, Rajavi tried to win the legitimacy abroad that he had lost at home, but now that the war is over, he is merely a pawn in the hands of Saddam Hussein.

With this failure, what remained of our people's traditional fascination for the romantic aspect of absolute power vanished. The people lost their respect for the Pahlavi-style dictator, the so-called reformer, exterminated by the Americans like a mouse. And they now have no more esteem for Khomeini, the former religious dictator, nor for Rajavi, the failed Stalinist. Like a curtain falling, these three failures have smashed the myth of absolute power.

A SOCIETY BLOWN APART

Things became even more complicated when ideological battles between modernist and traditionalist mullahs were joined to the existing Left/Right political divisions. Problems arose when the mullahs realized that the value of science, technicians, and experts had to be acknowledged. The antagonism increased when Khomeini proclaimed that music was no longer banned, that it was all right to play chess, and that women could sing. Activities the mullahs wanted stopped were suddenly permitted—and during Khomeini's lifetime, yet! Society was a mass of cracks; the war had convulsed structures and psyches. Feuds with the Bazaar over nationalization had exacerbated the socio-economic malaise. Corruption, already widespread, became the national pastime, spurred by unemployment, rising prices, and decreased output. Immense networks were organized, with as many as five hundred people involved in illegal activities in every economic sector, not to mention the drug rings. In the civil service, groups were formed to speculate in urban real estate, passports, foreign currencies, antiques, carpets. Under the heading "Miscellaneous Items," the newspapers regularly announced five hundred to a thousand arrests. Corruption spread to foundations supported by the regime, with the Right condemning the shady dealings of the leftist foundations and vice versa. Recently, we learned that an organization claiming the Koran as its only capital had performed billions of monetary transactions.

Ration books have been in use since 1984. Everyone receives coupons to buy meat and staples. A black market has developed for these coupons, which certain groups print and sell. *Le Monde diplomatique* revealed in April 1986 that $10 billion belonging to the mullahs was deposited in American banks; and on July 4, 1986, *Le Nouvel Observateur* gave the name of the woman—Tina—who manages these billions of dollars, not to mention investments in Japan and other countries.

People jokingly say that Iran has become self-sufficient in four things: drugs, video cassettes, boutiques, and prostitution. International-scale mafias have been formed with the Italians, the Afghans, and the Lebanese. Some people in Iran believe that Olaf Palme was assassinated by one of these mafias because he wanted to halt Sweden's secret arms sales to Iran.

This war also upset our way of life. Statistics published in November 1985 revealed that 25,000 of the 55,000 Iranian villages had become ghost towns, 19 percent of them had no more than twenty-five households, and 15 percent had only ten to twenty-five. This exodus, already noted during the Shah's reign, accelerated. The war tore the Iranian family apart by creating political, ideological, and social divisions between its members. Families were also scattered, with one child on the front, another in exile, a third in the black market. The family home became a center of conflict, made worse by the cost of living and, frequently, by bereavement. It is impossible to say how society will evolve, but nothing will ever be as it was before. The status of women, for example, has changed totally, despite the mullahs' repression. Women have become active members of society, in addition to their role in the family.

Schools have also become a battleground between a government intent on controlling everything and a society anxious to escape such control. The family and the school are quite often at odds, with families trying to give their children an alternative education to counteract the official teaching of the clerics. Violence and the use of drugs have increased considerably. For many, they are the only way of escaping social constraints.

Religious institutions are faltering since they no longer completely dominate social life and Khomeini betrayed them by deciding that politics must take precedence over religion. Change is possible, but only if the political institutions succeed in freeing themselves from control by the mullahs. This political supremacy statement of the Imam's is perhaps the first step toward a new

Iran. Khomeini was forced to take this crucial step by the change in the people's behavior toward Islam and the mullahs.

The economy, drained of vitality, is adrift. Nationalization has failed, as has liberalization under the mullahs' iron rod. The effect of all these disturbances has been the creation of a situation beyond the regime's control. Social groups such as unions and professional associations have disappeared. The last union—that of the physicians—was abolished in 1988. The mullah-controlled Islamic organizations within the government exist in a vacuum. Only the neighborhood associations survive, half underground.

I believe that all dictatorships end as ours has. But if, in our case, everything is so obvious, it is because the mullahs' ideology is rooted in the past, whereas Stalinism and fascism contemplated a radiant future for mankind.

Social movements have sprung up intermittently in the last few years. Obviously, it would be an exaggeration to say that the masses are on the move, but there are signs. Even within the regime, references to the founding principles of the revolution are now becoming increasingly frequent. Some even go so far as to say that Montazeri—by espousing freedom, independence, and progress—has become the new Bani-Sadr. Violence, a cardinal value in the Islam of the early years of the dictatorship, now plays a much smaller role in the regime's propaganda. With the gradual collapse of the principles supporting dictatorship, the regime has been overpowered by the idea of peace, a process made more urgent by the country's political and military constraints.

The question of war or peace having been resolved, problems crucial to Iran's future have resurfaced. Consequently, the newspapers have been full of articles about progress, independence, and freedom—whether compatible with Islam or not. The force of circumstances has brought about a return to the revolution's principles; it may also be the way to exorcise the recent past.

I am pleased to see these changes, and I know that I have contributed to them through my writings and, since going into exile, through my denunciation of the collusion between the mullahs and the Reagan administration. Irangate was the perfect opportunity to make myself heard. True, the Lebanese newspaper revealed the name of Robert McFarlane, Reagan's emissary to Iran, but I collected a great deal of information, which I disseminated both in France and in the United States.

CONTACTS BETWEEN KHOMEINI AND BANI-SADR

A few months before Irangate, Khomeini wanted to renew contact with me. I received his first messenger early in the summer of 1986. He was instructed to say only that I was missed in Iran. I replied that regret without action changes nothing. The messenger then asked who I would accept as a regular emissary from the Imam. I suggested looking for someone not connected with the regime, someone who could function as a tape recorder and be content simply to carry messages.

A second overture was made just before the massacre in Mecca. Khomeini's wife sent me a friendly note, saying that we should forget the past.

Members of his family also related his comments to me on several occasions, particularly when Mousavi and Khamenei went to him to settle their differences. He told them, "The two of you together are not worth Bani-Sadr's little finger." In an interview for an Arab magazine, *Hadi Khosroshahi*, a mullah who is also Iran's ambassador to the Vatican, said that in a meeting with the Imam (who was upset about Irangate and my criticism of the regime) he had suggested that I be assassinated. To that Khomeini replied, "Why kill him? He's a Muslim."

Later, messengers ran back and forth constantly between Tehran and Paris. The tenor of Khomeini's messages changed after our initial contact. At first, he wanted me to write a letter setting forth my demands. I refused because it would have been both a powerful means of exerting pressure on me and an acknowledgment of his legitimacy.

I therefore asked him to go before the people to proclaim a return to the letter and spirit of the revolution, which have been lost from sight since the people expressed their will in the first presidential election. I said that only a shock of this nature could create a national and international climate favorable to Iran's emergence from an impossible situation. He asked me to come back to work with him toward freedom. I answered that all freedoms must be restored before I could consider returning.

He proposed amnesty and the legalization of political parties. I agreed, of course, but it was not enough. I still demand the restoration of three basic freedoms: speech, assembly, and political parties. When this step has been taken, I will decide. Until then, I will wait. Continuing executions, purges, and political assassinations are ominous signs and justify my hesitation.

20

KHOMEINI SWALLOWS THE POISON OF DEFEAT

IN 1985, GENERAL PESSIMISM CONCERNING A MILITARY solution to the war overwhelmed both the population and a large majority of the political officials. The human wave tactic could not continue. At this time, 57 percent of the Basij were school children. It was impossible to continue sending children to the front without incurring the wrath of their parents. The bombing of our cities and the repeatedly broken truces exhausted the population. Iraq had been in complete control of the airspace since June 1985, and its economy was better able to support the war because Saddam Hussein had been able to normalize oil exports.

After the human wave tactic, military officials again tried the guerrilla technique of breaking through the enemy lines at random points, but the volunteers for martyrdom were becoming increasingly scarce. After Irangate, the Revolutionary Guards began asking questions. For whom was the war being fought— the United States or Israel? The impact of Irangate on the morale of the combat forces was devastating. In early 1986, the taking of Fao in Iraqi territory restored a bit of hope, which was quickly extinguished. Until Irangate, and even afterward, Western experts, fully aware of the recruiting problems in Iran, still thought that Iraq could not last for long, that the technique of zigzag advancement would eventually succeed, and that sooner or later the Iranian troops would cut through the lines and open the road to Baghdad. Saddam Hussein knew that reinforcing his army was the only way to prevent this disaster. In response to Iraq's urgent request, Egypt agreed to send workers to make up for the labor shortages caused by the war, but not soldiers. It was then that he decided to use chemical weapons. An important thing to realize about chemical shells is that, to be effective and to minimize the risk to the user, they cannot be dropped from airplanes; they must be shot from guns, which necessitates the adaptation of strategies and tactics to this type of warfare. In 1987, the Iraqi army mastered the handling of these devastating weapons. Who provided them with the equipment and the technology? The Soviets and Germans supplied the plans and training, and the French sold them 40 percent of the guns. All hope for an Iranian military victory vanished.

To have said, in 1987, that the war was lost for the Iranians would have been true, because of the chemical weapons and of the army's other handicaps: the logistical problem, the lack of unity at the command level, and the poor discipline and training of the Basij. It used to be said in Tehran, as a sort of macabre joke, that the Basij, like ammunition, were made to be used only once.

In September 1987, the Iraqi army was in a strong position and could very easily have retaken Fao, but Saddam Hussein carefully refrained from doing so to show the Arab world that Iraqi territory was still occupied. The series of Iranian attacks on Karbala on the fifth, sixth, and seventh ended in failure. The last offensive in Shalamsheh, for which enormous forces were assembled, was equally ineffective.

On April 16, 1988, the Iraqis retook Fao in thirty-six hours and then went on to recapture the rest of their territory occupied by Iran. In June, Khomeini's troops withdrew to the north, and in July, after the acceptance of Resolution 598, the Iraqis entered Iranian territory. Today, officials of the regime claim that a thousand square kilometers of Iranian territory are occupied by Iraq.

•

THE DIPLOMATIC YO-YO

Since they had lost all hope of a military victory, the mullahs sought rapprochement with the Americans and the Soviets. True to the spirit of Iranian diplomacy since the Kajar era, the mullahs played yo-yo with the two superpowers to extract the maximum benefit from each. The ties between the Khomeini regime and the Reagan administration are long-standing and date from the hostage affair, with signs reappearing in the following years as well, such as when the mullahs cooperated with the British and the Americans in connection with the Soviet spy assigned to Iran who defected to the West. In May 1985, the Saudi foreign affairs minister came to Tehran to discuss a potential Arab-American plan to oust Saddam Hussein, which came to nothing. Claiming that it was time to face reality, the Right then proposed turning once more to Israel, the only country able to pressure the United States into supplying arms on a large scale.

Surprisingly, the Khomeini regime cooperated with Right and far Right groups all over the world, because many mullahs believe it to be the only way of obtaining satisfaction from the West. In September 1985, for example, a plane departing Tabriz strayed into Israeli territory before returning—loaded with spare parts; and on September 14, Benjamin Weir, an American clergyman held hostage in Lebanon, was released. In this same period, Rafsanjani told his associates that if he did not succeed in ousting Saddam Hussein with American help in the next six months, he would lose his life. Obviously, he was in contact with the Reagan administration concerning arms, of course, but also regarding a political deal—Rafsanjani offering to guarantee American interests in the region if the United States forced Saddam Hussein from power.

To counter this drift toward the United States, the Iranian navy stopped and inspected an American ship in the Gulf for the first time in January 1986. The pro-Soviet faction hoped to block contacts with the United States by provoking it. Surprisingly, one month later, in February, Gorky Markovich Kurnenko, secretary of state for foreign affairs in the Soviet Union, visited Iran for the first time to discuss Caspian Sea oil, the export of Iranian natural gas to Soviet Russia, and the war, of course.

•

After McFarlane's visit to Tehran on May 27, 1986—which was revealed by the Hashemi group—Rafsanjani temporized for a time to avoid a frontal attack on the pro-Soviet faction. The Americans returned to Iran in September, but then, two months later, Irangate erupted.

As Shimon Peres said in November 1987, oil can no longer be considered a weapon against the West. This meant simply that the Americans had succeeded in transforming relations between the West and the countries of the region and had regained control of OPEC. That being the case, why not try to get along with the Iranians? The climate in America seemed to favor detente. In December 1986, for example, the Heritage Foundation, an organization with close ties to the Republican Party, mentioned a prospective rapprochement with the Khomeini regime on four points, which also served as the basis for relations between Rafsanjani and George Bush, the American vice president. They were: organization of the oil market, stabilization of the regime, the release of political prisoners, and an end to the Iran-Iraq war as an investment in the American elections in 1988. Since February 1988, these points have been the Bible for relations between America and the Iranian Right.

In this same period, Khomeini, who on principle always had two irons in the fire, maintained close relations with the Soviet Union. He had some difficulty in this regard, however, since in June and September 1985 the Russian experts left Iran, ostensibly because they no longer felt safe with Iraqi missiles falling on the cities, but in reality to exert economic pressure.

In January 1986, Gromyko harshly criticized Iranian policy during a visit to Moscow by Saddam Hussein. The thaw set in eight months later with the signing of the natural gas and Caspian Sea oil contracts. I protested, asking the government if it intended to replace the Shiite belt with a red belt—Syria, Iraq, and Iran all jumping on the bandwagon. But I knew very well that the Soviets would not try anything while they still had Afghanistan on their back. In this period, the mullahs even went so far as to ask the Soviets to organize nothing short of a coup d'état in Iraq.

The conflict between the regime's two factions was bitter. While in November Khamenei was telling the secretary general

•

of the United Nations that his government would demonstrate greater flexibility with regard to the ceasefire, the other side scored a victory with the Soviet oil agreements, to which the Right replied by violently attacking the Soviet Union as the supplier of chemical weapons and missiles to Iraq.

One way or another, they tried to frighten one of their partners into giving them something; then they did the same to the other. The Rafsanjani group brought things to a head in February 1988 by waving the specter of a potential leftist alliance with the Soviets, which would turn Iran into another Ethiopia. Khomeini's emissary tried to communicate this fear to me by telling me that the Mousavi government was planning a coup with the Soviet Union and that the recent bombing of Saddam Hussein's birthplace had been organized under instructions from the KGB. I never considered this possibility, but I knew that the plan existed.

I was already convinced that neither the Soviets nor the Americans would permit an Iranian victory, and that since their rapprochement on November 21, 1985, in Geneva, they had decided to act jointly. On April 3, 1986, the *Herald Tribune* published a report prepared by twelve American, Indian, and Soviet experts recommending the neutralization of Iran. As if by chance, a short time later, in July 1986, Itzhak Shamir declared that the West ought to normalize its relations with Iran.

On January 24, 1987, however, Reagan warned the Khomeini regime about the war shifting to the Persian Gulf, and in May, Kuwait asked the UN Big Five to provide protection for ships in the Hormuz Strait and beyond. In this affair, the Arab world united against Iran and resolutely declared itself in favor of American intervention. The crisis with the Gulf countries, kept alive by the regime's left-wing, made the presence of the U.S. Marines possible.

THE FATAL BLOW

The massacre in Mecca in August 1987 was another blow to the people's morale. There was talk at the time of a plan to impose peace that would have been a sort of Hiroshima for Khomeini. Mecca would be the first stage and the Iranian airliner shot down over the Persian Gulf by an American missile the coup de grâce. This is also how Rafsanjani, in July 1988, justified his sudden decision to honor Resolution 598 of the UN Security Council. He described the shooting down of the airliner, which left nearly 290 dead, as the precursor of other catastrophes if Iran did not immediately agree to the cessation of hostilities.

The history of this resolution is indicative of the Iranian regime's retreats and Khomeini's hesitations. In February 1986, Iran rejected a resolution calling for a ceasefire and the opening of negotiations. In January 1987, the foreign affairs ministers of the five permanent members of the Security Council began meeting regularly. Their thirteenth meeting ended with a plan that the Security Council approved in July and adopted as Resolution 598. It called for an immediate ceasefire, withdrawal to the border, and a team of UN observers to monitor compliance. This was to be followed by the exchange of prisoners and the opening of negotiations between Iran and Iraq on every aspect of the conflict.

The Iranian regime immediately rejected this resolution, which was unfavorable to it, to say the least. The tension mounted, and U.S. Secretary of State George Shultz, speaking on behalf of the Five, threatened Iran with a blockade if it did not accede to the resolution.

The Iranian position softened very quickly. On August 11, 1987, the government demanded that Iraq be designated as the aggressor and that reparations be paid. This was definitely a step forward.

In October, the Iraqi and Iranian delegations attending the 78th Interparliamentary Conference in Thailand voted in favor of a motion calling on the warring parties to implement Resolution 598 quickly.

Throughout this period, Khomeini remained silent. He was sulking because he knew that the die was cast, that his mullahs had accepted the ceasefire. Since 1985, he had allowed Rafsanjani to work toward ending the war politically, but he had many misgivings because the end of the war in the existing circumstances

•

would have been a defeat for him. When Rafsanjani's aides came to discuss the ceasefire, Khomeini answered, "Over my dead body." He said the same thing in June 1988 to two clerics, Golpahegani and Marashi. A few days later, however, he was confronted with a fait accompli. According to another story widely circulated in Iran, Rafsanjani was working with Khomeini all along and they split the roles to allow themselves a way out.

At this time, in mid-1988, the Americans were very anxious to end the war. Moreover, a peaceful breeze was blowing through all of the world's trouble spots. Seven of the wars being fought at the time had the following in common: they were of long duration, the superpowers were involved, and none of the combatants won a decisive victory. These were the wars in Lebanon, Afghanistan, Angola, Cambodia, Nicaragua, the Iran-Iraq war, and the Arab-Israeli war. The American elections slated for November had a lot to do with this frantic quest for peace.

On July 20, 1988, Iran accepted a ceasefire.

Parliament, meeting immediately in a closed session, refused to ratify the agreement presented by Rafsanjani, but he cleared this obstacle by calling to the rescue several members of the Assembly of Experts, the commanders of the armed forces, the prime minister, and several of the regime's dignitaries who approved the ceasefire but had no power to sign treaties. The next day, Rafsanjani went to see Khomeini to give him the text of the agreement. Extremely dejected, Khomeini declared publicly, "I have sold my honor; I have swallowed the poison of defeat."

In the days that followed, the regime's pro-Soviet faction ran back and forth to Syria, but to no avail since the process of rapprochement with the United States was too far advanced to be challenged. Khomeini had gambled heavily on Bush's winning the American elections.

Tongues started wagging after July 20. First, Kissinger wrote in *Newsweek* that his plan had succeeded, and then on July 22, *Le Monde* informed us that in March, Velayati had told Genscher that Iran was going to accept Resolution 598. The day before, Michael Ledeen, a Reagan adviser, declared in the *Los Angeles Times* that Iran had agreed to the resolution months earlier and that Iraq was dragging its feet because Saddam Hussein wanted to recover his

territory before acceding. The *Sunday Times* that day added that
the ceasefire stemmed from an agreement between Bush and
Rafsanjani concluded in February.

As expected, the Americans profited from both the war and
its conclusion. Everyone, including McFarlane, had to put in their
two cents' worth to say loud and clear that Khomeini had
capitulated.

21

CONCLUSION

TWO YEARS AGO, IN TEHRAN, EHZATOLLAH SAHABI, FORMER planning and finance minister, stated that $105 billion of the last ten years' oil revenues had vanished into thin air. The country's records vouch for the expenditure of only $45 billion of the total $150 billion in oil revenues. In the same period, the government borrowed the equivalent of $200 billion from the national bank. The regime, in desperate financial straits, is trying to obtain loans.

In 1988, the Iranian government needed $17 billion in foreign exchange to finance its imports. According to the most optimistic figures, oil and other exports brought in no more than $7.6 billion, leaving a deficit of nearly $10 billion.

The war is not the only reason for this. The reverse oil crisis and the U.S. recovery of control over OPEC have sharply reduced oil producer revenues. By the late 1970s, the producing countries had increased their oil revenues by $288 billion. In 1987, they fell $95 billion. This loss of income is a great blow to the economies of the producing countries, especially Iran, which, to survive and to meet the needs of its people, must sell its oil at auction.

Currently, the Iranian family earns a third less than it needs, whereas in 1980 it earned a great deal more. The result, according to official statistics, is that 72 percent of the Iranian people live below the poverty line.

To prevent protests and social unrest, the government, no longer able to use the war as a safety valve, has stepped up repression, already an integral part of daily life in Iran. Not long ago, Larijani, then-deputy minister of foreign affairs, questioned by a German reporter about the new round of executions, responded, "The birth rate in Iran is very high; each year the Iranian population increases by two million." This appalling comment went unnoticed; no one in the Federal Republic of Germany or anywhere else objected. This reminds me of an anecdote Khomeini once told me, which is still relevant today. One day, Khalkahli, then a deputy, came to ask Khomeini to make him prime minister. Khomeini smiled and said, "As a matter of fact, as prime minister you could settle the unemployment problem by executing half of the population." Hitler killed to increase the Germans' *lebensraum*. Khomeini killed to create and expand the mullahs' living space.

The repression and daily executions in all of the cities are dreadful proof that the people have not been brought to their knees. The mullahs' despotism is being met with a resistance which, although unarmed, is nonetheless fierce. Playing a leading role in this resistance are women, who have achieved a new social status. They have been forced into action by the mullahs, who ordered the wearing of the *chador* before revealing the enormity of their thinking: "Woman is the symbol of the devil and of death, a sexual object who must not appear unless covered from head to toe." According to this definition, the role of women is limited to the rearing of future martyrs. Women were very quickly relegated to one of two categories: those who would not submit and who incited society to rebellion, and the rest, dutiful women, suppliers of cannon fodder.

The mullahs quickly realized that the way to control society was to control women. Thus, women suffer greater repression. In the name of Islam, executioners torture, imprison, and execute women who, for the most part, live in accordance with the Koran. This situation is unprecedented in the history of Iran. Women of all social classes have not only refused to let their children die but have also supported the youth freedom movement.

•

CONCLUSION

•

The Iranian people's resistance to the structures imposed by the mullahs is especially encouraging since the recent trend in international relations has been toward liberation of the oppressed. The overthrow of a number of totalitarian regimes in the Third World and the course of events in the Eastern bloc and in the industrialized countries, which apparently have understood that development must benefit everyone, are some of the reasons why I feel optimistic. The restoration of freedoms in Iran would have decisive consequences because, in addition to occupying a unique geopolitical position in the world, Iran is the cultural heart of the Islamic world. If this heart stops beating, despotism and corruption will continue to rule the Muslim world.

Perhaps the days of despotism in Iran are numbered.

The repeated failures of the Shah, who admitted that he had been tossed out by the Americans like a dead mouse, and those of Khomeini, who admitted having swallowed the poison of defeat, perhaps herald a new era in Iran's relations with the superpowers. Irangate, the first scandal between the American colossus and a Third World country to have had significant repercussions in the political life of the United States, is surely an important factor in this evolution.

The proof? Reagan, when questioned about the restoration of the monarchy in Iran, replied, "After Khomeini's death, the existing organizations will try to change the country, each in a different way. The people are aware of this, and the United States will support any government that restores freedom and democracy."

With yesterday's supporters of the monarchy now advocating a democratic process in Iran, and with Montazeri, Khomeini's designated successor (who was dismissed by Khomeini just before his death), declaring that the only solution to the present crisis is the restoration of freedoms, it is clear, barring other obstacles, that Iran's political future is mapped out: it is democracy.

Was I naïve throughout this entire period of history? I think not. At every moment of his political life, Khomeini applied the following Machiavellian principle: "Any act is good if the politician can employ evil instead of good, falsehood instead of truth, without being detected."

•

219

In Machiavelli's time, culture was at a low ebb and the role of the people was insignificant. Today, the consciousness of the people grows day by day and political actions must conform to this growth. The language of truth must replace that of deceit if the people are to have confidence in their leaders. This is what I achieved when I was in power. For the first time since Mossadegh, a public official spoke the unassailable language of truth.

Like everyone else until then, I distrusted political power, but I had enormous confidence in religious counterforces. Was this naïve? I do not think so. It would have been naïve to think, as Khomeini did, that despotism can be good or evil; that the Shah, because he was evil, betrayed his country, and that he—Khomeini—because he was good and above reproach, would act in society's best interest.

When I, the first elected president in the history of Iran, was forced to choose between power and freedom, my choice left not even a shadow of a doubt. Although I am often asked to do so, I refuse to return to my country while it is chained to the yoke of despotism. It is not I who must return to Iran—it is freedom.

INDEX

INDEX

•

•